Rural Women in India

Published by
Saurabh Publishing House

Rural Women in India

Dr. Manjula Sen

Saurabh
Publishing House
4735/22, Prakash Deep Building,
Ansari Road, Daryaganj,
New Delhi- 110002

Published by :
SAURABH PUBLISHING HOUSE

Distributed by :
Lotus Press Publishers & Distributors
Unit No. 220, 2nd Floor, 4735/22, Prakash Deep Building,
Ansari Road, Darya Ganj, New Delhi- 110002
Ph.: 41325510, 09811838000
• E-mail : lotuspress1984@gmail.com
www.lotuspress.co.in

Saurabh Publishing House is an imprint of
Lotus Press Publishers & Distributors

Rural Women in India

ISBN: 978-81-89005-29-0

Preface

Women in India are seen as a burden to society, not an asset. In developed countries, women have proven their worth by standing alongside men and working jobs, earning money, helping to feed their children, and even making important scientific discoveries. In India, though, this rarely happens, if at all, outside urban areas. Women in rural India are seen as property. When a girl marries into a family, she works for her husband's family's welfare, not her parent's welfare. Although dowry has been illegal since 1960, parents of a female child usually have to pay dowry to the other family so they will allow her to marry one of their sons. This happens more in rural areas than in urban areas.

Almost 750 million people live in rural areas, and this is where caste systems, female discrimination, and female infanticides are at their strongest. In rural India, the only wealth women can depend on is their offspring, which causes a strong desire for male children. Unfortunately, this is reflected in the alarming statistic that female infant mortality figures are 40 per cent higher than male. Females are more likely to be aborted than males because of India's strong preference for male children. Since male preference is adamant in India, women are more likely to be bereft of medical attention, food, and education. When women lack education, they are more likely to have more children, as children are their future financial security.

The hunger situation in India is poor at best, and it is even worse for women. In recent years, India has been able to reduce hunger to one-fifth of the population, but sadly, one-half of preschool children are malnourished, and most of them are girls. In India, rural, poor women are generally the most disadvantaged. There is blatant discrimination against women, and this proves to be a major barrier against creating a hunger-free India. In order to reduce poverty, hunger, and rapid population growth, women must gain equal rights, including more education opportunities, and the right to own property.

This book explains and analyses the multifaceted and multidimensional role of rural women in India's socio-economic life. Topics such as the status and contribution of rural women, efforts made by government for upliftment of women's status etc., are elaborately discussed. The lucid explanation, critical analysis and objective evaluation of facts will be highly useful for academicians, policy makers and executors, who are actively working for the development of rural women.

Author

Contents

	Preface	*v*
1.	Status of Rural Women	1
2.	Gender-based Discrimination	39
3.	Rural Women and Education	69
4.	Rural Women and Health	103
5.	Rural Women and Employment	139
6.	Socio-economic Development of Rural Women	161
7.	Women's Political Participation	193
8.	Rural Women Empowerment	229
	Bibliography	265
	Index	269

1

Status of Rural Women

In India, about three fourth of the population, still live in rural areas. The notion that women in rural societies enjoy relatively higher social status appears to be a myth. Gender discrimination is a social reality irrespective of the nature of societies and no universally applicable rule exist to measure the degree of status of women in various societies. There is an imperative need to delineate the factors determining the social and economic status of women and to make efforts to strengthen the process that help women to raise their status in the society through educational, political and economic empowerment.

According to the 2001 census, the sex ratio for India's population is 1,072 males per 1,000 females. This ratio is significantly higher than those of neighbouring countries: Pakistan (1,066), China (1,059), and Bangladesh (1,049). For India, though, the 2001 ratio indicates a slight improvement from that observed in the 1991 census (1,079). This gain can be attributed to better health facilities for women and, to some extent, to improvement in the status of women. But any complacency over this development must be tempered by the fact that there are sharp differences across states. While Kerala has a sex ratio of 945, Haryana's ratio of 1,161 reflects considerable gender imbalance. It is unclear whether the cause for this imbalance is out-migration of the male labour force in Kerala and in-migration of male workers in Haryana or systematic use of sex-selective abortion.

Today almost 1.1 billion people live in India, comprising one-sixth of the world's population. So far, only China has a more populated country, but that is estimated to change within the next 45 years. China only allows one child per family, but in India, there is no such limitation, and families have many children, especially poor families. The average number of children per family in India is 2.73, but in extremely poor areas such as Bihar, there is an average of 4.3 children per family.

Another cause for population growth is lack of use of birth control. Only half of the population uses some form of birth control. If women were more educated, they would be more willing to use birth control, but in rural areas, females are not given the opportunity to continue schooling after they are 10 years old. The hunger situation in India is poor at best, and it is even worse for women.

In recent years, India has been able to reduce hunger to one-fifth of the population, but sadly, one-half of preschool children are malnourished, and most of them are girls. In India, rural, poor women are generally the most disadvantaged. There is blatant discrimination against women, and this proves to be a major barrier against creating a hunger-free India. In order to reduce poverty, hunger, and rapid population growth, women must gain equal rights, including more education opportunities, and the right to own property.

Throughout India, there is no particular lifestyle shared by all, or even most, but there are common traditions among Indian households. Households usually consist of extended families, though families with just parents and children are becoming more popular, especially in cities. After marriage, the bride goes to live with her husband's family. The new bride has the lowest status in the family. About 5,000 estimated deaths occur each year in India from supposed "kitchen fires", but the correct term is "bride burning". These cruel incidences happen because the bride's family cannot afford the dowry requested by the in-laws, which can be both excessive and subject to increase after marriage. Bride burning is a result of pure greed, and demonstrates women's unequal status in Indian society.

Among India's poor population, domestic abuse is more common. Because of a high desire to breed males, women are subject to violence and torture by the in-laws if they do not produce males. For most families, male children are the priority, because they will support the parents in their later years, when the parents cannot support themselves financially. A couple may have a large number of children in the pursuit of a male child. If female children were considered as valuable as male children, then families would not need to produce a large number of children in hopes of producing a male.

A smaller family means more food per person, and the children have a better chance at being properly nourished. If females were considered equal to males, dowry would no longer have any purpose, since in-laws demand dowry because the bride cannot work and earn money like the husband can. Without dowry, there would be no purpose for bride burning, and bridal abuse would eventually become nonexistent.

At least one third of the population of India, most of them female, does not get adequate nourishment. Traditionally, the men and children are served first, and what is left is eaten by the women and older girls. When families have little food, there might not be any food left for the women, which leads to severe undernourishment. When families do have food, they often consume grains, fresh fruits, and seeds of pod vegetables. Since most of

India is vegetarian, they must find other ways to get nutrients other than eating meat. A study conducted in the city of Vadodara in Gujarat state showed that 75 per cent of adolescent girls were suffering from anaemia.

Any physical activity would tire them quickly, even an activity as easy as walking a short distance. It was also hard for them to concentrate. UNICEF immediately established a programme to deliver red tablets consisting of iron to the girls. The programme was installed in 426 schools in Vadodara, affecting 69,000 girls. Within 18 months, anaemia had gone down by 22 per cent, and haemoglobin levels had gone up by 75 per cent.

The girls were able to study better, exercise without fatigue, and they no longer felt weak during menstruation. The programme has since then been expanded to all 25 districts of Gujarat, covering 950,000 girls. Although this is an enormous success, it is overshadowed by the fact that Gujarat is one of the better off states in India, and it raises an alarming question as to how many other girls in India suffer from anaemia, especially in poorer cities.

According to the United Nations, 500 million Indians live on less than two dollars a day. Because of India's sheer size, per capita income is a disappointing 3,300 dollars. Since women are discriminated against frequently, female workers in rural India earn 10 rupees less a day than males, even though they are working the same job. Not surprisingly, women turn to procreating to secure their future. Every year 18 million people are added to the country's population. This produces a strain on the health and happiness of domestic families.

Another result from the population boom is shrinking average farm sizes, which have decreased from 2.7 hectares to less than 1.6 hectares, as the land is divided among the children. Farms in India produce rice, wheat, coarse grains, cereals, milk, tobacco, bananas, and pulses.

The Green Revolution increased food production in India significantly, but educating women in India is the best way to keep increasing food production, and to restrain the increase in India's population. Unfortunately for India, many companies miscalculated the market size and have huge capacities of idle products, which have turned India into a buyer's market, instead of a seller's market. This is a setback for India's economy as they cannot make enough profit on their products.

The education for women in India is a major problem. After turning ten, half of India's children discontinue school. Because children receive little formal education, illiteracy is a major problem in India. Today the literacy rate is a measly 64.8 per cent. Female education is imperative to raising the income of Indian families. If mothers are educated, then child nutrition improves dramatically. A study in Peru revealed that seven or more years of schooling for women reduced infant deaths by 75 per cent.

An analysis completed in 2000 showed the connection between malnutrition in preschool children and uneducated mothers. The best way to reduce hunger is to educate the mother. Educated women have fewer children, leaving more money and resources to spend on each child. The mothers can earn money to provide more resources for the children.

The solution, then, begins with education. Education for women is the best way to improve family health and nutrition. If women have no opportunities for paid jobs, then they are dependent for their sole wealth and security on their offspring, especially the male children, and this consequently produces high birthrates and puts a strain on food supplies. With education, women are prone to marry later and have fewer children. This is a real benefit in a world crowded by people, and limited in resources.

Education helps women's self-esteem and status in society.

In Mexico, where a recent study was conducted, women said education had been their ticket into a higher social standing and security for them and their children if their marriage failed. Education had dramatically improved their lives, and their happiness. If such an idea created so much success, why would it not produce the same effect across the ocean in India? How can this goal of more educated Indian women be accomplished? Since girls make up half of the youthful population, the "international community should resolve to invest its influence and resources in improving the educational, medical, economic, and political opportunities for girls".

The World Food Programme sees that 90 per cent of food is produced by women, but women only own one per cent of the farmland. The reason for this severe imbalance is that women cannot secure a loan from a bank to start a business or buy farmland. Banks need collateral and can only find it with landowning men.

Other problems, such as rapid population growth, can be solved by educating women in India. If women are seen as equals, then they can work and be paid as equals, taking off the pressure to procreate several children that would take care of the mother in her old age. Urbanisation affects food production as well. The World Bank estimates that each year one million workers move out of agriculture. This is undoubtedly linked to India's annual urbanisation rate of 2.4 per cent.

As Indians move out of rural areas into urban cities, slums and shanty towns surrounding a mega city continue expanding and growing. Severe investments in urban infrastructure need to be implemented such as water, sanitation, food supplies, and transportation. As India's food production grows, more people should move to urban areas because fewer farmers are needed. As a result, food prices fall, and more people are persuaded to move to a city.

Urbanisation helps economic growth by creating more acres per farmer as other farmers move into urban areas. People are attracted to urban areas because of higher wages. Sparsely populated rural areas and densely populated urban areas make the most sense for increasing economic growth. Once the majority of the labour force is no longer engaged in food production, then it is natural that more people move into urban areas. Urbanisation can be a good thing for India, if urban infrastructure is improved for the people moving in from rural areas.

Another way to combat overpopulation is to educate women in birth control. Only one-half of the population uses some form of birth control. Six out of ten women who choose voluntary sterilisation wait to do so after they have at least two male children, with an average of four children in all. Indians do not have a problem with birth control because of religion. They are suspicious of birth control because they are poor, illiterate, and uninformed.

In 1976, forced sterilisation was implemented in poor areas to combat overcrowding. The people were told that their chance at receiving money or a job from the government increased with a certificate of sterilisation. The government was essentially dangling a string consisting of food and money in front of these people, and the people could have it as long as they went through a difficult and life threatening procedure.

A 1993 study showed that 67 per cent of contraceptive use was female sterilisation with only nine per cent male sterilisation. This fact simply does not make any sense. Why should the government force women to be sterilised instead of men, when the procedure was infinitely more dangerous, difficult, and deadly for women? If a procedure can entail death, and the procedure is the only option for birth control, then it is no wonder why Indians would opt to not use contraceptives at all. Fortunately, since then, Indians have become more aware of the system and are fighting to change it. Couples in India need to be educated on birth control, all forms of it, and be given options other than female sterilisation.

Adult women must be given opportunities to become entrepreneurs. Already in Mumbai, India, this concept is starting to take place. A man named Abraham George, bought 50 acres of barren land in one of the poorest areas of India, not to make a profit, but to fight the problem of poverty and hunger. In this part of the country, 75 per cent live below the poverty line.

There is also a strict caste system in place, a high number of female infant deaths, and little rainfall. Abraham says, "It is the perfect place to start". After four years and another 150 acres, the farm has become the second-largest banana farm in South India, with 200 families employed, and its land value has tripled. Abraham's major goal in India is to empower rural women.

Chetan Ahya, an Indian economist at Morgan Stanley, says, to significantly change the poverty stricken Indians, the "government and productive public sector (need) to help rural Indians earn money and be schooled". Meanwhile, Abraham George continues to help poor single mothers earn money and own land. An Indian woman named Rajamma borrowed 4,000 rupees from a landlord and had to enslave herself and her children until the debt was repaid. Social workers from George's farm came looking for poor women to work at the farm, and Rajamma was one of them. They paid Rajamma 40 rupees a day and set aside money to help her buy her own farmland (Bray). This is one of the many ways people are making a difference for women in India. Attitudes toward women must change.

Throughout history, because women bear and raise the children, they have not been expected to need an education or to obtain a job. They were considered to be the property of the men in their family, whether father or husband. As people become educated in the developing world, they begin to realise that women can do more. If there is birth control, the woman is not forced to produce so many children. If there is education, she can raise the family's standard of living. If the laws allow her to own property, she can provide more resources for her children. The world has been reluctant to treat women as equal human beings. After all, it has been less than a century since women in the United States have won the right to vote. Encouraging women to become educated, to limit their family size, and to seek economic freedom, will contribute to India's rise out of poverty and hunger.

On the path to creating a hunger free India, it is imperative that women be considered equals, receive more education, and achieve the right to own property. This will not happen if the world does not focus its energies on this problem. Funds need to be provided for schools allowing females to continue on past primary school. Women should not be discriminated against when receiving medical care. The international community should work together with India to solve anaemia in adolescent girls. Iron tablets should be distributed since they significantly increase the girls' ability to concentrate and exercise, and the tablets make them feel stronger.

Urban infrastructure needs major improvement as more people move out of rural areas and into urban centres. As food production increases, the number of farmers per citizens should decrease, creating more land and resources per farmer. Food relief should be distributed to the mother, instead of to the father, because the mother is more likely to use it to feed the children. Child malnutrition goes hand in hand with uneducated mothers. Education for females significantly improves a child's nutrition. Good nutrition is the basis for a good future.

Family planning should be taught to every family. All forms of contraceptives should be available to Indian couples. Couples should be able to choose whether or not to use birth control and what forms of it to use, once they are educated about it. The couples should never have unwanted and dangerous operations forced upon them. For India to impede population growth, people must be educated about birth control and be offered options. To combat poverty, women should be given the opportunity to work for money and own businesses. If women were offered the same salary and job opportunities as men, then they could be a source of income for the family.

India has a huge population problem, and educating women would be the deciding factor in reducing the population in coming years, since women are less likely to have many children if they are educated and have the ability to compete in a job market with men. The international community must help women in every way, so women can soon be considered equal to men. Ultimately though, it is up to India whether or not she will let women become equal partners in the global solution for world hunger.

FUNDAMENTAL RIGHTS OF WOMEN

The Constitution of India guarantees equality of sexes and in fact grants special favours to women. These can be found in three articles of the Constitution. Article 14 says that the government shall not deny to any person equality before law or the equal protection of the laws. Article 15 declares that government shall not discriminate against any citizen on the ground of sex. Article 15 (3) makes a special provision enabling the State to make affirmative discrimination in favour of women. Moreover, the government can pass special laws in favour of women. Article 16 guarantees that no citizen shall be discriminated against in matters of public employment on the grounds of sex. Article 42 directs the State to make provision for ensuring just and humane conditions of work and maternity relief. Above all, the Constitution imposes a fundamental duty on every citizen through Articles 15 (A) (e) to renounce the practices derogatory to the dignity of women.

All these are fundamental rights. Therefore, a woman can go to the court if one is subjected to any discrimination. When we talk about constitutional rights of women in India, we mainly pertain to those areas where discrimination is done against women and special laws formulated to fight those bigotries. The most important issues stand as those pertaining to marriage, children, abortion, crimes against women, and inheritance. Before modern Hindu laws were passed, child marriages were the norms, inter-caste marriages were banned, the girl became a part of the husband's family, and polygamy was common.

In the 19th century, the British rulers passed several laws to protect customs and traditions while abolishing detestable practices like Sati. Some such revolutionary laws were Hindu Widows Remarriage Act 1865 and the Brahmo Samaj Marriage Act 1872, the forerunner of the present Special Marriage Act. In the beginning, the Act sets four essential conditions for a valid Hindu marriage. They are:

— Monogamy,

— Sound mind,

— Marriageable age,

— The parties should not be too closely related.

Polygamy was permitted among Hindus before the Act was passed in 1955. However, after the act was passed, any man marrying again while his wife is living will be punished with fine and imprisonment up to seven years. Formerly, child marriages were common. The Child Marriage Act of 1929 was not very effective as such marriages were continued to be performed. Now, however, the bridegroom must be 21 years old and the bride 18 years. However, there is a separate Muslim Code of Conduct, which allows polygamy of up to four wives as per Islamic laws. A marriage may be invalid without the boy or the girl realising it at the time of the wedding. A civil marriage would be void if four essential conditions are not complied with. These conditions are listed in the Special Marriage Act, as enumerated below:

— If it is bigamy,

— If either party was suffering from mental disorder,

— If the boy has not completed 21 years and the girl 18 years,

— The boy and the girl are too closely related, or in legal language, are "within degrees of prohibited relationship" unless custom governing at least one party permits the marriage between them. Prohibited relationships are listed in he Special Marriage Act.

— A fifth reason for invalidating a marriage is impotence of either party.

There are some grounds available to the wife only, both in Hindu and civil marriages. One such ground available exclusively to the wife is her husband's commission of rape, sodomy or bestiality. Under the Hindu Adoptions and Maintenance Act 1956, a Hindu wife is entitled to be maintained by her husband. Section 125 of the Criminal Procedure Code also deals with maintenance of wife and children. If there is a decree of maintenance against the husband and the couple have been living apart for over one year, it would be a ground for the wife to seek dissolution of marriage. Here again the Muslim Personal Law has a different set of conditions for the annulment of an Islamic marriage.

The Dowry Prohibition Act of 1961 says that any person who gives, takes, or abets the giving or taking of dowry shall be punished with imprisonment, which may extend to six months or with fine up to Rs. 5,000 or with both. Dowry that started off as a practice to give away presents to the departing daughter, usually some resources to begin her new married life, slowly assumed extraordinary proportions and turned into a social evil. Brides were expected to bring the "gifts" regardless of their personal willingness. The bride's family could no longer have an individual say; lists were prepared and sent to the girl's house before the final agreement between the two families.

The condition being that the boy would marry the girl only if the demands were met. Such a custom is being practiced not only in India but also in other countries like Bangladesh and Nepal. The reason behind this custom is the poor economical condition of the people along with a lack of education; unawareness of legal rights among women and a general bias against the women. Crimes like rape, kidnapping, eve teasing and indecent exposure can be grouped as crimes against women. Rape is the worst crime against women after murder and the maximum punishment under the Indian Penal Code (IPC) is life imprisonment.

An abortion or miscarriage due to natural causes is not an offence. Therefore, the law does not deal with it. However, violent and forceful abortion is a crime.

Sections 312 and 316 of the Indian Penal Code deal with abortion as crime. Section 313 deals with abortion without the consent of the woman. The punishment could even be life imprisonment. The Hindu Succession Act gives male and female heirs almost equal right to inheritance. Section 14 says that any property possessed by a female Hindu shall be held by her as full owner and not as a limited owner.

WOMEN'S ECONOMIC CONTRIBUTION

Although most women in India work and contribute to the economy in one form or another, much of their work is not documented or accounted for in official statistics. Women plow fields and harvest crops while working on farms, women weave and make handicrafts while working in household industries, women sell food and gather wood while working in the informal sector. The informal sector includes jobs such as domestic servant, small trader, artisan, or field labourer on a family farm. Most of these jobs are unskilled and low paying and do not provide benefits to the worker. More importantly, however, cultural practices vary from region to region. Though it is a broad generalisation, North India tends to be more patriarchal and feudal than South India. Women in northern India have more restrictions placed on their behaviour, thereby restricting their access to work.

Southern India tends to be more egalitarian, women have relatively more freedom, and women have a more prominent presence in society. Cultural restrictions however are changing, and women are freer to participate in the formal economy, though the shortage of jobs throughout the country contributes to low female employment. But in the recent years, conditions of working women in India have improved considerably. More and more women find themselves in positions of respect and prestige, more and more workplaces are now populated with women who work on equal terms as men. Working is no longer an adjustment, a mere necessity; but a means to self worth and growth.

Women have now not only found their place in work places but are also party to governance. In recent years there have been explicit moves to increase women's political participation. Women have been given representation in the Panchayati Raj system as a sign of political empowerment. There are many elected women representatives at the village council level. At the central and state levels too women are progressively making a difference. Today we have women Chief Ministers in five large states of India. The Women's reservation policy bill is slated to further strengthen political participation.

Important Legislation

Today Indian womanhood is marching towards liberty and equality. For this march towards liberty and equality, various social legislation passed from time to time are mainly responsible. This legislation aimed at eradication of social evils. Following are the significant enactment, which helped in bringing about the change:

- *The Hindu Widow Marriage Act of 1856:* In the traditions Hindu society there was a ban on widow remarriage. Ban on widow remarriage was one of the most important evils from which women in the traditional Hindu society suffered a lot. This Act allowed widows to remarry and section 5 of this Act ensured her to enjoy all the rights which a married woman did.
- *The Child Marriage Restraint Act of 1929:* The practice of child marriage was another social evil from which woman in traditional Hindu society suffered a lot. Age at marriage for girls was 9 or 10 and after passing this Act the minimum marriageable age of

women was fixed to 15 years. Later it was increased to 18 years.

- *The Hindu Women Right to Property Act of 1937:* In traditional society women had no property right. In the eyes of law she was minor or ward. This Act recognised a widow of a deceased person as his surviving personality with the same right as his in the joint property. Thus through this Act women in the Hindu society received the property right to a limited extent.
- *The Hindu Marriage Act of 1955:* This Act has recognised the equal rights of man and woman in the matters of marriage and divorce. Under the provision of this Act either the man or woman can present a petition in a court of law for divorce, wife has got an equal right to divorce her husband as he can do.
- *The Hindu Succession Act of 1956:* This Act recognised an equal right for women in the matter of inheritance of property. She can inherit the property of father along with her brothers. She can also sell or mortgage the inherited property or use it for herself. For the first time absolute ownership was conferred to a woman by this Act.
- *The Suppression of Immoral Traffic in Women and Girls Act of 1956-57:* This Act aims to deal with the problem of prostitution and to promote the welfare of fallen women. Main objectives of this Act are to reduce the scope of prostitution and to reform the prostitution under this Act. Every state is expected to set up protective homes and to appoint women police and women social workers. In protective homes these fallen women will be given training in tailoring, toy and basket making and other crafts so that they may earn for their maintenance in a proper way.

— *The Dowry Prohibition Act of 1961:* The main objective of this Act is to abolish giving and taking dowry at the time of marriage. The term dowry refers to a valuable property or thing which is determined by the parties to a marriage for a marriage. The practice of dowry had produced very bad effects. Dowry has become a social evil. Even though this Act prohibits dowry system, the dowry cases have not been reduced. Still this Act makes some effort in bringing social change.

Above mentioned are the important legislations which brought upward trend in the status of women in India. Today what women are enjoying their status is because of legislations. She is protected in every way of life. Thanks to legislations, women in India are gaining better status, recognition and respect.

STATUS OF WOMEN IN ANCIENT INDIA

Throughout ancient history, women were obliged to abide by the laws made by men. However, it is also true that vedic society had a number of women in key positions and that certain austerities could not be performed without their wives even in the early ritualistic period. In fact according to legends Lord Brahma was forced to take up a girl named Savitri as his consort for a special worship, in the absence of his wife Saraswati. The ritualistic vedic culture was indeed male dominated. Women folk only helped in the preparation of things for the rituals and fire sacrifices and did not conduct rituals themselves.

Intellectual Revolution followed as the fire sacrifices of the vedic culture was challenged by thinkers including women, who speculated on the nature of religion. In search of salvation, they confronted the profound mystery of death. Their quest predicted on two principles—

Renunciation and Karma, the individual's position in *samsara* (worldly life) determined by one's past actions. During this period woman scholars took active part in spiritual discussions and were also much venerated as seen in Upanishads. Some of the women scholars were more knowledgeable, dominated the scene and were highly respected. Buddhism and Jainism which had limited but enduring appeal were the two major developments of this Intellectual Revolution. Many of its first converts were Vaisyas (merchant class), affluent urban group, upwardly mobile, and, women, both of whom wanted to overcome the low ritual status in the dominating ritualistic Hindu society.

During Vedic age, women gained a high place in the society through their own efforts. There was a period in which great many changes were taking place in Sanatana Dharma itself, which absorbed the alien spiritual practices and customs from pre-vedic cultures. Sankara, founder of Advaita philosophy (non-dualism) noticing the danger of mass exodus from Sanatana Dharma to Jainism and Buddhism established six traditional forms of worship in which Devi (Goddess) worship was given equal importance along with vedic and non-vedic forms of worship like the worship of Ganesha and Kumara. He composed several hymns in praise of Devi—Soundarya Lahiri, Kanakadhara stotra, Annapoorneshwari stotra etc.

Vedas are also full of prayers for the birth of son. Brihadaranyaka Upanishad elaborates ceremonies for the birth of a son. Some of the wedding blessings start with "Be the mother of the males". Side by side vedic society encouraged Devi worship, recognised and acknowledged superior intelligence wherever existed as in Kenopanishad glorifying Uma. Vedic society then did not disturb that part of the society that gave prominence to female supremacy under its fold. Their policy had been live and let live within the fold of Sanatana Dharma.

The mention of Women sages like Vaac, Ambhrini, Romasa, Maitreyi and Gargi in vedic lore collaborates this view. Mythology talks only with high respect about the three consorts of Brahma, Vishnu and Shiva and countless ladies like Ahalya, Anusuya, Arundhati, Savitri, Lopamudra, Sakuntala, Damayanti etc. Hinduism had several mystics like Andal and Avvai of Tamilnadu, Mahadevi of Karnataka, Lalla of Kashmir, Chellachi of Srilanka, Janabai and Muktabai of Maharashtra and Mirabai of Rajasthan. At present Amritanadamayi of Kerala is well known in the USA.

Women could undergo the Upanayana samskara (ritual) and pursue vedic studies. They were known as "Brahmavadins". Those who did not pursue the path of the brahmavadins were called "Sadyovadhoos". Co-education existed in the earlier period. Ladies of Kshatriya Dharma got training in the use of arms and other martial arts. Both Kanya-vivaha (marriage of pre-puberty girl arranged by parents) and "Praudha-vivaha" (marriage after puberty) were prevalent. Under certain circumstances the girl had the freedom to choose her husband. The wife known as "grihini" was considered as "half" of the husband and constituted the real "griha" or home. She was called "saamraajini", the queen or mistress of the home and had an equal share in the performance of religious rites.

Saastras prescribed sacraments exclusive to woman to honour the coming of puberty and motherhood like Pumsavanam, Seemantonnayanam etc. Divorce and remarriage of woman were allowed under special conditions. Vesyas (prostitutes) were allowed to make a living in the society, but were regulated by a code of conduct specially made for them. Mythology shows that women were allowed to have more than one husband. One of our much respected mythological women Panchali was married to five Pandava brothers. The Atharvaveda says that a woman can marry after having ten husbands. Another respected woman of India, the mythological Tara, who came out of the Ocean of Milk, married Vali, the monkey king and after his death married his brother Sugriva. The fisher woman Satyavati had a son by Saint Parasara and later married King Santanu and had two more sons.

For a fairly long period women dominated the social scene and were the virtual head of the family while men were busy with their nomadic life and hunting pursuits. Due to constant threat from foreign invaders and also the draught situation of the Saraswati-Sindh belt the population moved to the East Gangetic plains where agriculture was vigorously followed to a large extent giving up nomadic life of early population. Some anthropologists think that rule by women preceded rule by men and that the patriarchal system developed only when men settled down to agricultural life so as to leave women free to bring up family. As the Great Goddess rules the heavens, her earthly counterpart, the woman, settled down to rule the home. It is no wonder, Manu, the law giver said, "The gods are satisfied wherever women are honoured, but where they are not respected, rites and prayers are ineffectual". Hinduism believes even today that a woman who devotes her entire life to the well-being of her husband is a "Pativrata" and is endowed with numerous powers usually attained by sages and it is said that even Gods can't match their power.

In the Tantra philosophy the female aspirant is looked upon as an embodiment of Shakti and is worshipped through rituals like Kumari Puja (Virgin worship) and Shakti Upasana (Goddess worship). Among Shaktiates women are always treated with great respect. Kumari puja is mostly conducted in Bengal. In this ceremony, a twelve year old girl from a Brahmin family is installed on a *pita* (a stool), dressed up like the image of Shakti and worshipped accordingly. Agricultural pursuit changed the society again in which the father, instead of the mother assumed the role of the head of the family. Western historians over emphasised this fact of the period and wrote that women were obliged to abide by the rules of men. This shift could have taken place when the population got settled giving up their nomadic pursuits, to work on farms and agricultural lands while the women managed the household with many children.

In their previous nomadic life, families were small with limited number of children and women had sole control of the family. Lot of research has gone into the status of ancient and medieval arts like temple sculptures, cave paintings, fine arts and ancient tradition, in which status of women indicates occupying a prestigious position. Hindu aesthetic tradition in the ancient and medieval times regarded women as an aspect of the Great Mother of all life, a vessel of fertility and life in full sap.

The ideas of Indian art viewed every woman, a Goddess. This has a parallel to the Great Greek Goddess of Fertility Gaia, the Earth, with mountains, caves and earth's waters considered as a woman and a Mother. Ancient art in many forms and old traditions reveal the true history on the Status of Women in ancient and medieval India. The ancient traditions of India have always identified the female of the species with all that is sacred in nature. It is not always the warrior woman who is identified with the Goddess, but also a woman as playful, lovable, and of course as the mother.

A kick of a woman was sufficient and necessary for blossoms of spring time from the sacred Ashoka tree. An entire ceremony has developed around this theme. Women dance around this tree and gently kick to bring it to bloom. By her mere touch the fertilising power of woman is supposed to be transferred to the tree, which then bursts into flowers. All things that arise from the earth in the form of vegetative life mirror the great generative function of the Goddess. The female figure is an obvious emblem of fertility because of its association with growth, abundance and prosperity. A tree that has come to flower or fruit will not be cut down; it is treated as mother, a woman who has given birth.

The metaphoric connections between a tree and woman are many and varied. A relevant one here is that the word for flowering and menstruation is the same in Samskrit. In Samskrit a menstruating woman is called "Pushpavati", "a woman in flower". It is interesting to note that the decoctions made from the bark of the same Ashoka tree, are used to soothe menstrual cramps and excessive blood loss during menstruation as recommended in Ayurveda. The bark decoction relieves the pain and tension related to menopause. Vedas consider river as the primordial womb.

Any kind of creativity of bestowing of life seems to evoke a symbolism of motherhood. This explains the common practice of calling the rivers "mother" a custom which is most noticed in the case of river Ganges but common to many other rivers as well. This correlation explains the common practice of calling rivers as Mother Goddess. This shows the high respect given to motherhood and woman in Hindu practice. Ancient art texts known as Silpa Shastras confirm that the potency of woman's fertility and its equation with growth, abundance and prosperity led to women becoming a sign of the auspicious. In fact, women served as apotropaic function whereby their auspiciousness was magically transferred to the monument upon which they were sculpted and painted.

A royal palace, a Buddhist Stupa, Hindu shrine gained auspiciousness and fortune when adorned with the figure of a woman. A text of the tenth century, the Shilpa Prakasaha, that provides guidelines for practicing temple architects and sculptures categorically states that figures of women are a pre-requisite on the walls of temples. Its choice of phrase underscores the significance of the theme—"as a house without a wife, as a frolic without a woman the monument will be inferior quality will bear no fruit". Thus by the mere addition of feminine images it was believed that the whole complex could become sacred and auspicious. In fact the same text lists the different types who best sanctify a monument and instructs the sculptor on how to exactly carve the figures. The most important of these feminine images are:

— a woman dancing;

— a woman adjusting her anklets;

— a woman drummer;

— a mother with her infant in her arms;

— a woman smelling a lotus;

— a woman playing with a parrot.

In ancient times, a woman dancer was considered an inseparable part of any ritual worship in temples. Every temple of consequence had attached to it one or more dancers. Such women were known as Devadasis. The sacred dancers were symbolically married off to the presiding deity of the temple. Thus an "ordinary" woman was found holy enough to be married off to God, the lord of the temple. The transformation of the ordinary girl into Devadasi was marked by important rituals, after the completion of which the woman was considered "an ever auspicious woman" (nityasumangali). The traditional view holds that all women, by their very nature, share the power of the goddess.

The devadasi initiation rites celebrate the merger of her individual female power with those of Goddess. It is this quality of 'eternal auspiciousness' in a woman that brought into existence this tradition since ancient times.

The importance of devadasis can be gauged from the fact that their presence was deemed necessary at the slightest event in the temple, for example bathing the deity in the morning or waving the sacred fire lamp in front of him. An important ritual was the participation in the twilight worship held at sunset.

The junction of twilight, when the day slips into night, is considered extremely dangerous, and so the gods need all the support and attendance they can get. The ritual of waving the lighted lamp by a devadasi was considered the most effective method of warding off inauspicious state for the divine. Dance of course remained their most accomplished contribution; indeed the life of a devadasi required a strict adherence to dancing schedule and practice. Dance is potentially both sensual and hypnotic. Its passion performance helped to evoke the atmosphere of temple as a place removed from the mundane world, the temple as a celestial abode of the deity. Even mythology does not look down upon celestial dancing girls like Urvasi, Menaka and Rambha who got into all sorts of problems time and again.

The relationship of the body, senses, mind, intellect and soul is articulated in the Upanishads and is seminal to the world view where body is regarded as the abode of the divine and the divine descends in the body. Logically, the body, beautiful is the temple of God and dance is a medium of invoking the divine within. Each form of dance—the stance, the movement and the context—is imbued with deep spiritual and symbolic significance. Dance reflects a state of being at the highest order of spiritual discipline (Saadhana) and is hence considered yoga. Its performance is a higher transcendental order. It is the medium which evokes the supreme state of bliss (Aananda) and also the vehicle of release (Moksha). Through the medium of dance, a woman embodies the progenitive powers of cosmic energy, through which, according to ancient dance treatise (Natya sastra) the entire phenomenal world is kindled to life.

The system in course of time degenerated to sex exploitation. The temple priest or someone in royalty would make devadasi lose her virginity. In the crudest terms she was forced to lose her virginity and was trained in erratic dancing. When a devadasi girl became a woman, she was allowed to wander around the country leading a life of prostitute. This abused system therefore completely abolished in India today. Wearing jewellery and adoring themselves with ornaments was natural to women in ancient days, as is today. Ancient texts identify sixteen different embellishments (solah singaar) which acknowledge and celebrate the beauty and divinity of the female form.

Sixteen, a significant number, corresponds to the sixteen phases of the Moon, which in turn is connected with women's menstrual cycle. A woman of sixteen is considered to be at the peak of physical perfection in her life. The image of woman adjusting her anklets in temple sculpture was considered sacred enough to be carved out in temple walls, though the Indian tradition thinks of feet as impure. A woman has no associated impurity, anything and everything connected with her acquired a status over and above its material existence. The anklet is mentioned as the last of these sixteen ornaments.

As mother, woman is divine and is worshipped. A mother with her infant in arms is found in all temple sculptural displays. A lady playing a drum is another common representation. A drum represents thunder and cosmic energy. Hide is a symbol of regeneration. Wood of the drum is symbolic of tree itself which expresses material nourishment and support. The hollowness of the drum inside is a symbol of the womb and therefore birth. The oval shape of the drum is a symbol of fertility, the feminine creative power. The lotus is the symbol of absolute purity; it grows from the dirty watery mire but it is untainted or unstained by it.

Indian literature classifies women into four types of which the highest is Padmini, the Lotus Lady. An early medieval text describes the goddess as being: "Slender as the lotus fiber; lotus eyed; in the lotus posture; pollen dusting her lotus feet. She dwells in the pendant of the lotus of the heart". The parrot is the vehicle of the God of Desire—Kama, the impeller of Creation. Kama is the God of Beauty and Youth. Creation is always preceded by desire; there can be no creation without desire.

In Nepal, A small Himalayan Hindu kingdom, a little girl is chosen to embody the Goddess for a few years, as the living image of Durga, as per the ancient tradition. Each year, the Kumari puts a Tika, i.e., a red auspicious mark on the forehead of the king, a gesture which signifies that she, goddess protects his legitimacy over the kingdom. Believe it or not, there have been communities in India, throughout its long turbulent history, where women have played important roles, in the society. For example, within the Nair community in Kerala, all property rites are only for women in the family, and they still follow the matriarchal system. In that system, the mother is always the head of the house. Shaving of the hair, wearing the red or white saree by the widows or their committing Sahagamana (dieing on the funeral pyre of their husbands) was never compulsory.

The sati custom seems to have been confined to a small section of the Hindu Society. The idea of shaving hair, perhaps was that their lives should be similar to that of Sanyasins, grihastasrama dharma having been snatched away suddenly from them. Sati according to leading Hindu theologisers had its roots in ancient Greece. Pyre sacrifices similar to Sati were prevalent among the Germans, Slavs and other races beside Greeks. Sati was never practiced in Southern parts of India. Even in North India it was practiced mostly among the warrior tribes called Rajputs who were descendants of Kushans, Saks and Partihans, who were constantly attacked by Muslim invaders.

The rare incident of Sahagamana from scripture's quote is the suicide of all the wives of Lord Krishna when this Avatar of Vishnu left Earth; it was voluntary and desperate out of extreme pains of perennial separation from their beloved husband. The other act in the Mahabharata parallel to Sati is the act of Madri, wife of Pandu, who killed herself on the funeral pyre, out of frustration and contempt for herself as she was the cause for Pandu's death. There is nothing in Vedas to show that vedic culture had sanctioned Sati. Sati has absolutely no Hindu scriptural backing. India had her own tradition of feminine culture and women's participation in spiritual and public affairs. From Sita and Draupadi of the Epics the tale ran through Rajput heroines to princesses like Rupmati of Malwa and Ahalyabai of Indore.

But by 1800 A.D. there was very little trace of feminine culture or public life; the less attractive aspects of the Hindu conception of the place of women in society portrayed predominantly by the Western historians and Hindu reformists were dominant. The new observers of Indian Society therefore found little to praise in the condition of women save their resignation and patient acceptance of suffering and much to criticise.

The targets of disapproval, though not all brought forward at the same time, were sati, infanticide, child marriage, the plight of Hindu widows, temple prostitution and forced dowry system. Ram Mohun Roy took up the fight against sati and infanticide in both of which the government intervened on general moral grounds. Swami Dayananda championed female education on vedic principles. The Ramakrishna Mission with its missionary techniques encouraged women teachers and preachers. Pandit Vidyasagar secured the First Act for raising the age of consent in 1860 and the legalisation of widow marriage. Child marriages were stopped in 1929 by Sarada Act under which no male is allowed to marry under 18 and no female is allowed to marry under 14.

Bankim Chandra Chattarjee mobilised women into the freedom movement, creating the character of Bharat Mata, Mother India, in his novel published in 1882, Anandmath. Bharatmata has much in common with Goddess Durga and is a favourite theme in Indian Nationalism. Subhash Chandra Bose and Mahatma Gandhi were convinced that a New India could be born only with women's full contribution and both invented new political roles for them invoking the goddess as an example for Indian women. Bose also gave a prestigious position to woman in the army in the role of Captain Lakshmi Saigal, who he compared to 'Shakti' and Rani Lakshmibai of Jhansi. Gandhi often drew explicit parallels, in his address to women, between Sita's legendary fight against the demon Ravana and Indian women's fight against British.

The earlier invaders, who came to India, looted, plundered and destroyed temples and marauding soldiers abducted young girls and women. As life, property and the chastity of women were at peril, each community built a fortress of social norms around itself to protect women. Caste system became rigid starting with the raids of Mahmud of Ghazni and Goris. Many later day social evils of the Hindus such as rigid caste system, guarding the sanctum sanctorum in temples from entry except by the few child marriage the forceful shaving of the head of the widows in higher castes, the wide spread practice of forceful Sati amongst martial race, became the norms during this unsettled period of Indian history.

Hindu women lost their independence and became objects requiring male protection. In the process they also lost the opportunities they had earlier of acquiring knowledge and learning in spite of the emerging philosophic schools of thought and reforms safeguarding interests of women, like Brahmosamaj, Veerasaiva Movement and Shakta Schools of Thought that still find place in Hinduism today. Veerasaiva cult flourished nearly 1000 years ago in the Karnataka region, stood for a casteless society, opposed child marriage, approved widow marriage and disapproved Sati. The Sovereign Democratic Secular Government of India is constantly struggling with its enacted laws, rules and regulations to safeguard women's interests.

In the face of economic constraints and rigidity of traditional customs and attitudes, the limits of political reformism are all too clearly revealed. There has been abundance of reformation legislations enacted and awareness of sex inequality seems to have grown at least within elite circles. The benefit which women as a group derive from the prominence of few women in leadership positions is insubstantial. The plethora of population, occupational, property and other legislations, has clearly upgraded the quality of many individual women's lives. But these changes are not indicative of any significant improvement in the status of women as a whole, which stands progressively degenerated to a large extent since the time of early invaders, especially amongst the low caste, illiterate and poor female population who are in a majority.

The slow progress in the improvement of the status of women after Independence due to social, political and economic impacts is being felt by the working middle class of the Indian community of which Hindu community is a majority. Right now in India, compared to even countries like USA, one can see women have better respect in social and political life as well as in professional life.

In India women have equal wages with men in all types of profession. A lady doctor gets the same salary a male doctor gets, and a lady engineer gets the same salary as a male engineer gets. In a society where woman have been progressively subordinated over a long period due to changing situations beyond control, this progress and presence of a woman Prime Minister or female chief ministers has not made significant land mark among illiterates, lower castes and the poor who are in majority. Much has been done and much more needs to be done to improve the literacy and economic and social conditions of women to bring back the past glory of Indian woman of ancient and medieval periods.

Status of Indian Women in Different Eras

Vedic Period: Literary and historical researchers have established beyond that the women held a position of quality with man during Vedic period. Both the girls and boys were imported Vedic studies. The importance of woman education is described in the Atharva Veda. It states," The success of woman in her married life depends upon her proper training during the Brahmacharya". In Vedic period, the women were so hymns of the Rig Veda.

In the Upanishadic period there were a large number of Brahmvadins who devoted their life in the study of philosophy. Gargi and Maitraye were two philosophers of prominence of that period. There were also great woman scholars during Buddhist period. Sanghamitra, the sister of the great emperor Ashoka, went to Ceylon to spread Buddhism. Ten married and 32 unmarried women were among the authors of Theragatha. Even in the Jainism period, the woman had an access to the education.

Yayant, princes, remained unmarried and received ordination from Mahavira himself. Based on these facts, Altekar writes, "We may therefore conclude that many girls in well-to-do families used to be given a fair amount of education down to about 300 B.C."

The marriage was looked upon as a religious and social duty. The unmarried person was looked upon as a religious and social duty. The unmarried person was not eligible to participate in Vedic sacrifices. This was not looked upon as compulsory for every girl. The matrimony was not compulsory for a woman and there was no limitation on the age of marriage. The women who remained unmarried and grew old in the house of her parents were called Amajur, a girl who grew old at her father's house.

The Vedic woman being grown up and educated had a voice in the selection of their husbands. Love marriages—Gandharva Vivaha were also common in Vedic period. Re-marriage of widow was permitted. The brother of the deceased husband could marry the widow with the permission of the elders. Some scholars are of the opinion that the widow could marry any person, not necessarily the brother of the deceased husband. According to Shakuntla Rao, the Rig-Veda does not mention anywhere the practice of the burning or burial of widows with their dead husbands."

In Vedic period, both husband and wife were joint owners of the property. Romeshchandra Dutt writes, Hindu woman held an honoured place... They inherited and possessed property; they took share in scarifies and religious ceremonies; they attended the assemblies and state occasions; they also distinguished themselves in science and leaving at their times... considered as intellectual companies of their husbands, as friends and loving helpers in the journey of life of their partners, in their religious duties, and the centre of their domestic bliss, Hindu wives were honoured and respected in ancient times." The position of the Hindu woman in the early Vedic times was much better than the status to which they were degraded about 300 B.C. The status of woman in Vedic period may be described as under:

The daughters were not unpopular in ancient India during the early centuries. They were allowed Vedic studies and were entitled to offer sacrifice to God. The son was not absolutely necessary for this purpose. The marriage of the daughter was not a difficult problem. The daughter herself used to solve it in most of the cases. There was no fear of widowhood because levirate (the custom of marriage of brother's wife) and remarriage were allowed by society and were even fairly common. The women before 300 B.C. enjoyed a high status and dignity.

Medieval Period: During the period from about 300 B.C. to the beginning of the Christian era drastic social change took place, which led to the curtailment of the freedom of women. Students of the Indian social history are of the opinion that the sons were valued more than daughter because the Aryans had a tough time of fight with tribal people who inhabited the Gangetic plains when the Aryans moved eastward from Punjab. In this way a desire for sons was created so that they could participate in the wars against the local tribals. An other thought is that there was great importance to ancestral worship than in the Rig-Vedic days. And as such, the sons were more valued than the daughters.

Some scholars are of the opinion that Upanishadic, Buddhistic and Jaina influence of asceticism is responsible for neglecting the daughters. The monks in search of the self alone relinquished all rites and renounced their homes. They also renounced their desire for sons, for wealth and for the worlds. They simply lead a life of beggar wondering from place to place. Consequently many young women renounced their homes and joined the Buddhistic and the Jaina monasteries. The life which some of these monks and the monasteries.

The one of the reasons of early marriage of girls was perhaps to prevent them from entering the monasteries as nuns. In due course of time the Aryans managed to over power non-Aryan people, i.e., local tribals. The Aryans married the non-Aryan women. There was no objection to such marriages but the non-Aryan women were prohibited from participating in the religious rituals. Initially non-Aryan wives were denied the right of religious sacrifies as they were not educated and the Sanskrit language was unknown to then. As time passed, Aryan or non-Aryan were denied the right of Vedic studies and religious duties.

The Upanayanam for girls became a mere formality. In the absence of education in the childhood, the girls were married soon after puberty. The Dharam Sastras declared that marriage was a substitute for Upanayanam, the neglect of education and lowering of the marriage age produced disastrous consequences upon the position and status of women.

The political condition also appears to have had their impact on the status of women. There were invasions during the period 300 B.C. to A.D. 300 by the Greeks, the Scythians, the Parthians and the Kushans. The political reverses, the atrocities due to war and the decline of prosperity, produced a detrimental effect on the society. The preaching of Upanishadism, Buddhism and Jainism started spreading and the status of widow was badly affected. Remarriage of widows was stopped and they were asked to devote themselves to and ascetic life at home.

The tonsure (shaving of head) of the widow was enforced by about the eighteenth century A.D. the *purdah* system was widely used in the middle class families. Altekar summarises the pathetic condition of women as, "Thus for nearly 2000 years from 200 B.C. to A.D. 1800, the position of woman steadily deteriorated though she was fondled by the parents, loved by the husband, remarriage, the spread of *purdah* and the greater prevalence of polygamy made her position very bad." There was a marked deterioration in the status of woman in the medieval period.

Modern Period: During the nineteenth and twentieth centuries, the status of women was improved by the untiring efforts of the following social reformers among others:

— Ram Mohun Rai (1774-1833),

— Ishwarchandra Vidyasagar (1820-1871),

— Dayanand Saraswati (1827-1883),

— Keshab Chandra Sen (1838-1884).

The important reason of the change in the social status of women in the nineteenth century is the acceptance of the tenets of liberal philosophy from the Western civilisation. It emphasised the principle of contract not the status, a rational outlook of life and its problems, freedom of speech, criticism of authority, authenticity of dogmas and insistence on the rights of man as opposed to his duties. For the first time in India, social legislation was enacted by the Government in nineteenth century. Rammohun Rai, informed Lord William Bentinck, the then the Governor–General of India that there was no mention of sati in the ancient Hindu religious books.

Accordingly, in 1829, he abolished sati and made it a crime. Ram Mohun Rai established Brahmasamaj and advocated the principle of freedom of women and equality of sexes. The untiring effort of Ishwar Chandra Vidyasagar promulgated the Widow Remarriage Act of

1856 and thus widow remarriage became legal. The great leaders of the nineteenth century saw the pathetic condition of thousands of child widows because of the practice of early marriage that was prevalent throughout the society.

In nineteenth century, Civil Marriage Act of 1872 was passed on account of courage and perseverance of Kashab Chandra Sen. This act made marriage a secular ceremony. The registration of marriage was compulsory; the age of marriage of girls was raised to 14 years. It also permitted widow remarriage and interacts marriage which was illegal up to that time the most significant feature of civil marriage Act was the enforcement of monogamy. The Hindu society accepted these great social changes of intercaste marriage and monogamy in 1956, after a three-fourth century.

The social reformers of nineteenth century also attempted to educate Indian girls. During the period from about 300 B.C. there was practically no education for women. Few women of the upper castes and upper classes had some education at their homes. The Dharam Sastra writers made women along with shudras ineligible for Vedic studies.

American Mission started a school for girls in Bombay, (now Mumbai) in 1824. In 1851 an Indian Society were formed to start girl's schools. The National Committee on Women's Education, 1959 says, "It cannot be denied that the general picture of the education of women was the most unsatisfactory and women received practically formal instruction whatever, except for the little domestic instruction that was available to the daughters of the upper class families". According to the Charter Act of 1813, the East India Company was entrusted with the responsibility of the education of the Indian people. Its efforts were restricted to the education of Boys and no effort was made for the education of girls as the Hindu society at that time prohibited it. The famous Wood Dispatch of 1854 reports:

— There were 65 girls' schools with 3500 pupils in Bombay Presidency.

— There were 256 girls' schools with 8000 pupils in Madras Presidency.

— There were 288 girls' schools with 7000 pupils in Bengal Presidency.

The rest of the country had very few schools. The Christian missions and the voluntary Indian bodies made a significant progress for the girl's education by the middle of the nineteenth century in comparison with hardly any education at the beginning of the century. The upheavals of 1857 as a result of the Indian War of Independence retarted the progress of education because the government adopted the path of religious as well social neutrality. In 1870 Municipalities were established, which helped to developed the primary education in India.

In 1870, training colleges for women were established for the first time for impoting training to the women so that they could become teachers in girls' schools. In 1882 the Education Commission recommended to open more schools for girls and to attract girls above twelve to the school education. It also recommended the appointment of women as teachers and inspector of girls' schools. The stipends were granted to widows who enrolled themselves for teacher training. By the end of the nineteenth century the women not only became teachers in girls schools, they also entered the profession of nurses and doctors.

The entry of women in professions indicated the marked change in the outlook of men and women in the last decade of the nineteenth century. Considering the progress made by the girls; education, it is beyond any doubt that the credit goes to Rammohun Rai who advocated for the women education in the beginning of the century. The nineteenth century may be called as a period of social change. In the beginning of the century, sati was prevalent and thousands of women were burnt at the funeral pyres of their husbands whereas by the end of the century, parents willingly sent their daughters to schools and also to work as teachers, nurses and doctors. There were several Indian women who worked for the betterment of the status of women.

Pandita Bai belonged to a learned Brahmin family in Karnataka. She attained the proficiency in Sanskrit language and she addressed many learned groups in different parts of the country, after the death of her parents she along with her brother travelled in the society, in 1880. She showed her boldness by marrying a man of a different caste and different language in 1880 after the death of her brother. After the Aria Mahila Samaj with the help of other leaders like Ranade and Bhandarkar.

Hunter Commission, after seeing the progress of Samaj in 1882, sent her to England where she was baptized as a Christian; she went to America in 1886 and returned to Bombay in 1889. She started a Sharda Sadan for the destitute high cast widows. The Hindu leaders objected to the conversion of Hindu widows to Christianity and as a result of which Ranade and Bhandakar left the Sadan; she shifted to Khedgaon near Poona and established Muktisadan where she gave general education and vocational training to thousands of women. There were many more outstanding women who contributed to the emancipation of women in the nineteenth century.

In the last decade of the century, Swami Vivekananda also gave a great impetus for the liberation of women from seclusion and bondage. He said, "That country and that nation which did not respect women have never become great nor will ever be in the future." He advocated the liberation of women and equality on the basis of the vedantic ideals that state. "One and the same self is present in all beings." According to him, the helplessness and dependence of women on men are due to the training given to her by men. In case she is not governed tyrannically her hidden power will make her a lioness. He emphasised that proper education will enable her to solve her problems and having independent thinking.

In 1917, Annie Besant, enlightened British women who settled down in India since 1803, launched the Home Rule agitation for the liberation of women. She was elected the President of the Calcutta Session of the Indian National Congress. In 1918 the Calcutta Session opined that the eligibility to all elective bodies concerned with the local Government and Education." In 1919 the Nagpur Session was attended by about 200 women delegates. This was also a striking evidence of the political awakening of the Indian women. Mahatma Gandhi encouraged thousands of women to participate in the political movement. Gandhi's fundamental faith in the equality of women was based, "on nonviolence, women have a much right to establish her own destiny as man has to establish his." He contradicted the preaching of Dharma Sastras for the injustice done to women. He expressed his opinion about the religious texts written after 300 B.C. that they advocate social inequality, promotion of child marriage and widowhood till death.

2

Gender-based Discrimination

Indicators of gender discrimination seek to go beyond description, and to identify policy measures for improving women's status or autonomy. Status has the connotation of relative social standing, and improving status may not increase autonomy, a term that suggests the ability of self-determination, independence and control over one's life. However, knowledge of status is important in defining norms of behaviour, and permissible deviations from such norms.

Demographic studies have tried to explore the extent to which women have control over their fertility behaviour by using various measures of 'autonomy'. Proxies used for female autonomy include female age at marriage, age difference between spouses, female secondary school education. An interesting dimension of autonomy, draws attention to the difference between autonomy that is culturally 'granted' and that which is sought. Most of the measures above reflect a social consciousness rather than individuality. Women do not 'choose' where to have their children, how long to stay in school, or when and whom to marry.

In fact, real autonomy in a majority of Indian households may be closely related to age, so that in a very real sense older women have the power to 'give' greater autonomy to young women. As Basu puts it, 'The real pity often is not that men wield so much domestic power, it is that during the prime reproductive years female power is at its lowest'. 'The 'socialises' rather than the already 'socialised' represent the potential agents of change'. There seems to be an increasing recognition in the literature of the interdependence of different variables. At the same time it is important to identify a single or a small set of interventions from which one could try and improve women's status/autonomy. The same variables may not be equally effective in all situations.

EDUCATIONAL SYSTEMS AND EMPLOYMENT

Education and employment are undoubtedly the most popular choices of ways to improve women's well-being. The cause of women's education, in particular, has received much support from the findings of demographers. 'A number of empirical studies indicate that the extent of anti-female bias in survival is substantially reduced by various influences that give women more voice and agency within the family. One of these influences is female education. Another is the ability to earn an independent income through paid employment. The schooling-fertility link has been found to be strong in all empirical studies, although the lines of causation are not always clear.

A recent study of Palestinian women re-affirms the power of education to secure better employment and economic independence and lead to more equitable gender roles. South East Asian experience also yields similar conclusions. The drawback of an excessive reliance on schooling as education is that usually it reaffirms gender roles and stereotypes; while formal schooling as a route to formal sector occupation is not substitutable, it is not always the case that educated and employed women are necessarily 'empowered' in the sense of having greater autonomy. Much depends on the content of the schooling.

In Eastern Europe, educational systems that favour learning by route have been compared unfavourably to those which emphasise problem solving. If independent critical thought is the essence of 'success' of schooling, this is by no means ensured in South Asian schools, with very few exceptions. Equally important is the number of years spent in school. There is scattered evidence to suggest that little difference is made to employment or other decisions unless 8-10 years are spent in school. However in India only 8.6 per cent of adult females, and 15.3 per cent of adult males have completed middle school, as against 40 per cent and 66 per cent who are literate. Moreover, even higher levels of formal education may be needed for the kind of exposure to new ideas and strategies that questioning of gender roles will need.

Employment as a route to empowerment is equally complex. Work participation levels of women are high, if an extended labour force definition is used, although the majority are in informal sector jobs, crowded into the low skill end of the spectrum, and usually in part time work. The uncertain impact of paid work on women's welfare is closely related to their continued home responsibilities. Does earning an independent income increase a woman's bargaining power? The answer is yes if she has real control over it.

In many situations however women work in response to household needs, and have been variously described as 'target earners' or as a 'flexible resource of the household'. It is unlikely that earning an income will alter the balance of power substantially; more likely, it will reflect the pre -existing balance of power in a household.

If this is reasonably good (a complex of individual and cultural attributes) work may be empowering; if bad, it can lead to higher levels of stress and continued exploitation.

In both rural and urban India, women spend a large proportion of time on unpaid, home sustaining work. With economic development many of these activities (fetching water for instance) should in theory be provided through public utilities or the market. At present these are still the responsibility of the individual. One estimate shows that 88 per cent of rural women and 66 per cent of urban women are engaged in one or another self-provisioning activity. Investment in infrastructure, specially the provision of facilities of drinking water, sanitation, and fuel and fodder, will result in a reduction of time on unpaid work. Other things remaining the same, this will contribute to an increase in women's welfare. But without any reduction in unpaid work, paid work is unlikely to be 'liberating'.

A second issue is that of labour mobility. Increased demand for women's labour, particularly in export oriented and labour intensive units, is a frequent outcome of structural adjustment programmes. But women may not be able to respond to new opportunities and to shift to new occupations, because their mobility tends to be low, even where migration is not involved. This is partly attributable to intra-household allocation of responsibilities. Rights and obligations within a household are not distributed evenly.

Male ownership of assets and a conventional division of labour reduce incentives for women to undertake new activities. In addition, child bearing has clear implications for labour force participation by women. Time spent in bearing and bringing up children often results in de-skilling, termination of long-term labour contracts, and in poor households can also result in deterioration of health. The behaviour of women in seeking work, and how entrepreneurial they are in the face of new opportunities, is also affected by the presence or absence of role models; so new jobs that get taken up by men easily get to be seen as the rightful preserve of men. Despite this, the East Asian economies witnessed a dramatic increase in women's labour force participation in the 1960s and 1970s. However, it is only where the labour surplus situation no longer exists, as in Singapore, that women workers in the export sector can be said to have distinctly better employment prospects subsequent to industrialisation.

Household needs change over the life-cycle, and women's labour force participation in different age groups shows varying patterns in different countries: single peaked, double peaked or plateau (as in India). The 'peaking' is caused by women dropping out of the labour force during the period that they have young children. Whether or not they return to work depends on labour market institutions as well as social supports and conventions. Studies suggest that women in the urban informal sector need to supplement family income once they have children, since it is not possible for the man to increase his earnings any further. Peak reproductive demands lead to an increased participation in paid activity, further increasing the vulnerability of women already at a vulnerable point in their life-cycle.

A clear distinction needs to be made between women whose work participation goes up in response to new opportunities and those whose work intensity goes up as a result of excessive demands on time. The latter is specially likely to happen to older women, who are not as mobile, usually illiterate and unskilled, who are unable to find alternative employment in a situation of restructuring. Such women may find themselves moving to less and less productive work, and longer hours, and probably increasing the quantum of unpaid work in an effort to save household resources. Greater mobility will benefit the one group but not the other.

Demographic Transition

While demographic transition has accompanied, or facilitated, economic growth in most countries, certain demographic characteristics that indicate the low status of women seem very resistant to rising incomes. Some preference that characterises India, and Asia in general, does not disappear with rising incomes. The discrimination evident in a declining sex ratio and in the large numbers of 'missing women' suggests that there is no reduction of gender bias in a context of economic growth. Indicators reflecting the health status of women show the same patterns.

- — First, the perception of poor health itself varies across gender.
- — Second, there is some evidence that medical intervention is sought more often for boys than girls.
- — Third, there is very inadequate allocation for health needs special to women.

The Cairo Conference on Population and Development recognised the need to address health and demographic concerns in a broader framework. The programme of action recognises the need for sustained economic growth in the context of sustainable development; education, especially for girls; gender equity and equality; infant, child and maternal mortality reduction; and the provision of universal access to reproductive health services, including family planning and sexual health.

Adequate investment in infrastructure and in social development characterised the growth of East Asia, and has been held up as a 'lesson' to India. Growth with poverty reduction has been shown to be possible. The poverty estimate in China in 1978 stood at 33 per cent and at 10 per cent in 1985. In Malaysia and Indonesia the poverty ratios continued to decline in the three or four years post reform. One common aspect of growth in these countries is investments in infrastructure and in health. But such investments are in themselves unlikely to be enough either to improve the relative status of women or to confront the patriarchal structures developed over centuries.

Conventional Indicators

How far do the above 'conventional' indicators succeed in capturing unequal gender relations? As one observer noted, 'Most of the world views Hindu women as degraded, downtrodden slaves. Yet the percentages of Indian women in the professions compare favourably with those of the West: Indian women comprise 7.1 per cent of the doctors, 1.2 per cent of the lawyers and 10.9 per cent of the scientists, in spite of incredibly low literacy rates for the overall female population...Clearly, Indian women present a paradoxical situation for the interpreter of South Asian society. The view of the Hindu woman as downtrodden represents one behavioural reality; her participation in the highest political and social arenas is another undeniable reality'.

Speaking on the subject of the changing position of Indian women in 1978, M.N. Srinivas was optimistic about the mingling of traditional support structures and new roles, concluding that 'migration to urban areas, female political participation, education, the activities of social reformers, and the inequities of dowry, all resulted in enabling women to make a relatively easy transition to new roles and responsibilities'. Among the enabling factors in this transition, Srinivas suggests that the availability of servants and of kin-networks are probably crucial in reducing conflicts between job pressures and home management. In addition, 'Indian men have not opposed feminine emancipation'.

One way of measuring the extent to which such a transition has taken place, from women being purely domestic entities, essentially playing a supportive role to men, to equal participants in economic and political activity, would be to look at measures of education, and employment. However the success of the transition will depend on its acceptability. If educated working women face high levels of stress, this may be the result of inadequate support structures and of low responsibility and emotional support from families. Measuring stress will require monitoring of less quantifiable indicators, including the degree of seclusion enforced upon women, domestic violence, and the prevalence of depression/ anxiety.

Domestic Violence and Depression

Domestic violence and depression are reported from very diverse societies. The form of the violence may vary, from dowry demands and bride burning to credible threats. Domestic violence needs a clear definition: it includes actual and threatened violence, psychological abuse and sexual assault, and its defining characteristic is that it tends to be repetitive in nature, but difficult to anticipate or avoid. The reluctance of women to acknowledge or address violence is hardly surprising, since it is usually associated with low self-esteem, a sense of personal inadequacy, and an erosion of coping strategies over time. Even more, family/kin are unwilling to acknowledge its existence unless it crosses some threshold level.

In a study of wife beating practices in Karnataka, Vijayendra Rao reports that 'Mild forms of wife-beating seemed commonplace. Many men and women admitted to it in informal conversations, often claiming that it was justified if the wife did not 'behave herself'. However, in the context of the survey interview, only 22 per cent of women admitted to have been physically assaulted by their husbands. Only the women for whom beating was a serious and chronic problem admitted to it.' And further, that 'Wife abuse, while widely tolerated and often even considered necessary by the community, has to happen under circumstances that are considered legitimate. Disputes over dowries, a wife's sexual infidelity, her neglect of household duties, and her disobedience of her husband's dictates are all considered legitimate causes for wife beating.

A husband who beats his wife when he is drunk, but is otherwise a 'good' husband, is also tolerated by the community, which believes that any sanctions they might impose would not have much effect on his drinking. However, husbands can suffer significant social disapproval when they batter their wives beyond levels considered tolerable by the village, or beat them for reasons not considered legitimate by the community'.

Violence is not unique to Indian or South Asian society, but the form it takes and the acceptable threshold, probably vary from one society to another. For instance, it is often remarked upon that Indian women may more often choose, even where economic independence is not the issue, to stay with or return to violent husbands, and in extreme situations choose 'suicide over separation.' The psycho-sexual basis of domestic violence itself is probably culture specific.

Without venturing too far into this field, some recurrent images which help to explain the persistence and acceptance of domestic violence in India, are reported here.

Policies and Interventions

Policies directed at eliminating or at least reducing gender disparities are an integral part of Indian policy documents today. The interactions between the various instruments are assumed to be mutually complementary. However, experience suggests that without adequate social supports, both psychological and physical, the outcomes are difficult to predict.

Education policies

Policy makers have generally been receptive to such goals as higher levels of education and employment. An emphasis on girls' schooling, hostels for working women, and other such measures increase opportunities for women within existing economic structures. It is also accepted generally that enhancing capabilities in this manner is not always possible through market mechanisms. A recent World Bank publication concludes that the persistent gender gap in education is an example of market failure and government action is needed here. In India, state interventions to promote access to schooling, work and health facilities take some note of constraints specific to women. But such interventions do not address the broader structural constraints on women.

Work

From observation and small samples, it does not seem that work outside the home increases women's agency, at least not on its own. In fact, clinical observation suggests that it can result in an increased risk of depression in women. The nature of the work, the extent to which women are in supportive relations, the presence of young children, whether husbands are employed or not: these are some of the many factors that determine whether or not work is beneficial or detrimental. It has been suggested that it is probably not the presence or absence of particular roles in women's lives that predispose some of them to more distress, but a particular combination of roles. There is evidence that multiple roles can be good for women's mental health.

Women who have several roles, but who also have social support and financial security, are less likely to get depressed than either women with few roles or sources of self-esteem/power, or those with multiple roles with many demands and little support. The central point is that developing economies are also changing societies. 'Western' notions of a mind at peace with itself include concepts of self-sufficiency, personal autonomy, efficiency and self-esteem; 'eastern' notions emphasise integration and harmony, social integration, balanced functioning and protection and caring. These make an impact on how one would treat the incidence of stress related disorders.

The western approach would emphasise control, understanding by analysis, problem solving and separation of body and mind. An eastern approach would seek understanding by awareness, acceptance, harmony, contemplation, and a body-mind-spirit unity. Therapy that takes the form of meditation or prayer may begin to have limited relevance where changing gender roles are involved. Or to put it in another way, a form of intervention is needed that can address both personal anguish and social/cultural oppression. This is a big task to undertake, requiring the development of 'a series of options, each one more socially connected than the last, in a progression from private symptom to public action'.

Law

In India, considerable emphasis has been placed on the law as a tool for social change. But how judges will interpret the law, and how far the intentions of social reform movements are translated into practice, is difficult to predict. Two decades ago, women activists did not hesitate to condemn dowry, or offer divorce as a way out of oppressive situations. Today, there seems to be a general feeling that no 'quick' solutions are possible, and that much more sustained action is needed. Dowry must be abolished, but women's rights to property must also be ensured. Divorce must be made possible, but the stigma attached to it must also go; women's ability to earn and live alone or to seek a new partner requires social consent and approval.

Counselling

It is here that institutions to provide support and practical alternatives acquire their importance. Today there are a large number of counselling centres in Delhi, for example, responding essentially to problems that arise in the wake of changing gender roles and aspirations, family structures and economic opportunities. An analysis of cases handled at the ISST Counselling Centre suggests that earlier patterns of arranged marriages are simply unable to cope with situations where personal initiative is needed and nuclear families are the norm.. At the same time marriages of choice between individuals from different castes/regions/cultures, which are becoming increasingly common, face even greater problems, with clashing cultural norms and role expectations that take a while to surface.

Social Networks

Autonomy for women should not imply irresponsibility

on the part of others. Hence the continued importance of support networks and group solidarity. Of relevance here is the distinction that has been made between the role of human capital and social capital. Empowerment of women, in the Indian context, unquestionably requires some change in the norms of behaviour. This in turn, calls for new structures providing emotional and psychological guidance, something that kin networks would normally do when norms are stable. The multilayered institutions that make up the social capital of a community do provide a fabric of support and a safety net for the vulnerable. However, while all societies permit some deviance, in transitional situations 'permissible' and 'actual' deviance come into conflict with each other. In devising development strategies that are sensitive to the need for greater gender equality, both the more individual route to empowerment (education, health, employment) and the 'institutional' route are potential tools.

STRUCTURAL ADJUSTMENT PROGRAMMES

Much concern has been voiced about the likely ill effects of macro economic reforms on the situation of women. Liberalisation has been seen to lead to increased feminisation of poverty. Privatisation has generated fears of reduction in state responsibility in the provision of social goods and services, resulting in an increase in the burden on women in the private domain to that extent. While increased feminisation of the workforce appears to be a global phenomenon, it has been pointed out that the increase in female work participation has been taking place in low-paying and unprotected jobs, leading to a rise in the casualisation of the female workforce. The main components of a structural adjustment programme are aimed at altering the long-run growth dynamics of an economy by operating on the supply side, while stabilisation measures are generally geared to reduce excess demand by curtailing deficits in external accounts and containing inflation in the domestic sector.

The usual package of structural adjustment measures consists of measures to allow greater 'free market' operations, free trade and enhanced convertibility of the domestic currency, privatisation and de-licensing of industry, reduction in tax and tariff rates, introduction of uniform rates of taxes and tariffs, abolition of price controls and subsidies and measures to improve labour market 'flexibility'. Stabilisation measures usually consist of domestic credit squeese, curtailment of budgetary deficits, reduction in money supply and devaluation. The impact of such macro policy measures on the gender distribution of costs and benefits both within and outside the market sphere is clearly not something that can be directly discerned or estimated. To a large extent it will depend on the existing scenario in gender equity to start with, and also the dynamics of changes in gender equations that may be propelled by the forces of economic reforms.

Although a number of authors have argued that the likely impact of these measures on women is predominantly negative, rarely have the lines of transmission of macro policy impact on gender balances in various spheres of activity been clearly demarcated or the complex of feedback impulses systematically contextualised within a proper format. If stabilisation measures usher in a recession, both men and women will suffer. Gender differentials of such suffering can be traced out only when it is contextualised within a particular socio-cultural milieu and it will be different under different contextual conditions.

Changes in the structure of employment, level and composition of social sector outlays etc. affect both economic and social arrangements. Gender relations are therefore likely to show some change, although as stated earlier, these changes are mediated by pre-existing conditions, so that outcomes can vary from one part of the country to another, and from country to country. Thus the propositions regarding the effect of reforms on gender discrimination detailed earlier are, in the present state of knowledge, simply a set of propositions, with mixed empirical evidence. Reforms would be judged as successful if they could eliminate poverty, and strengthen the processes of economic and social change that lead to increased welfare. An intrinsic component of greater welfare is higher status of women.

Although it is possible to justify interest in how gender relations might change with economic growth on purely economic grounds, this would be a narrow perspective. It is important to understand whether the pattern of growth being followed holds the potential for developing capabilities and enhancing the quality of life for all citizens. The intensification of work, discontinuation of education, increases in time spent on home maintenance, higher levels of stress and violence, are all ways in which economic re-structuring can affect women adversely. Using conventional indicators of equality, India's developmental experience has involved a gender gap.

According to the 1991 census, the male literacy rate was 63.9 per cent, as against 39.4 per cent for females; school enrollment as a percentage of the corresponding age group, was estimated at 108.8 per cent for boys in the age group 6-11, in 1985-86, and 77.1 per cent for girls in the corresponding age group; the difference in enrollment is greater in the age group 11-14, being 65 per cent for boys and 38.1 per cent for girls. This understates the actual gender difference, since attendance is far lower for girls, as observed in micro studies.

Despite the fact that women are biologically the stronger sex, an estimate of age and sex specific survival rates shows higher rates for males over females up to the age of 40, possibly reflecting inadequacies in nutrition inputs and care to young children/nursing mothers. However, there has also been an improvement over time. How much the improvement actually has been largely depends on the particular combination of indicators used. One attempt to measure the behaviour of the gender gap with economic development suggests that it is only in South Asia and in Sub-Saharan Africa that this gap increased in the two decades upto 1984.

The same study finds an inverted U pattern of rising gender inequality in the initial stages of human resource development and then a declining phase; the implication possibly being that labour scarcity forces higher investments and positive action to reduce gender bias. It has, at the same time, also been observed in India that even communities that traditionally paid a bride price upon marriage now demand a dowry; the incidence of 'dowry deaths' is widespread; and reports from family counselling centres suggest that role conflicts are high as is the incidence of depression, anxiety and domestic violence. Changing gender relations is tantamount to a questioning of established norms. As a consequence, this may be associated with increased violence, or threat of violence, and attempts to force a return to established norms, or at any rate to ensure that new norms do not radically alter the balance of power. Measuring gender discrimination in a situation of change requires tools appropriate to a dynamic context.

Determinants for Sex Selection in India

To understand the underlying determinants for sex selection in India, we will use a framework originally devised in 1973 by Ansley Coale for researching fertility decline. According to Coale, three preconditions needed to be met in order for birth rates to fall: birth limitation had to be within the "calculus of conscious choice" for parents; it had to be advantageous to them; and it had to be feasible.We will now adapt these prerequisites to the SRB scenario. These conditions can be translated into a simple matrix: parents should be willing and ready to practice sex selection, and also able to do it.

The first condition sounds straightforward, as the availability of the requisite technology is an indispensable ingredient for sex selection. There are different methods available, and each entails certain costs or limitations. Legal conditions may also act as a hindrance to sex selection. To a large extent, this latter component refers to supply-side factors, although this also needs to be widened to include non-material elements such as prohibitions or awareness factors. The second condition encompasses two aspects. First, this includes the ethical or religious context. As some of its ingredients (especially abortion) may be repugnant to them, parents may be unable to adopt them as techniques to regulate the sex composition of their offspring. The second aspect relates to what can be referred to as the rationale framework: parents will engage in sex selection only if they gain distinct benefits from their efforts. Even when sex selection is both acceptable and accessible, it may not be of any interest, as is seen in many parts of India where sexratio levels appear normal.

Basic methods

The following basic methods used to influence child sex ratios. But many other folk methods existed in the past, and are still reported today. These were probably of limited reliability, however, and unlikely to have left any tangible impact on India's sex composition. Of course, the dramatic technological breakthrough due to the introduction of ultrasound technology is probably the main cause for rising SRBs, but remnants of the old discriminatory regime have not completely disappeared. In fact, the existing sex differentials in infant and child mortality demonstrate that neglect, as an indirect method to eliminate "surplus girls", is still common. Moreover, the influence of new technology is far from complete, though government intervention has blocked the introduction of more "high-tech" methods of sex selection. As such, supply is somewhat crippled by current legislation, and may tend to lie below the actual level of demand for sex selection. Such a situation, of course, is likely to encourage criminal or other initiatives to circumvent regulations.

Traditional methods: One of India's oldest means used to alter the gender composition of children is also the crudest, i.e., female infanticide. The method relies on a set of procedures to kill girls within a few days after their birth. Techniques vary locally according to indigenous know-how and available resources. Such techniques have also evolved spontaneously over the years, incorporating newly available elements (such as pesticide). Infanticide's efficiency is beyond doubt, and its financial cost is also extremely limited because of its reliance on local resources. But this method also presents many drawbacks, especially due to the distress caused to mothers.

The huge psychological cost of female infanticide has subsequently made its use exceptional, and often limited to especially unwanted births. As a result, infanticide as a routine practice (and not as a last-resort solution) has never spread widely in India, as was the case in some East Asian countries, remaining instead restricted to a few communities, such as specific sub-castes in Western India or in Tamil Nadu. Lack of privacy related to matters such as pregnancy and delivery also tended to facilitate knowledge of infanticide, requiring both local tolerance and discretion in case of legal threats. Neglect is a far more common method. It consists of a passive strategy intended to deprive girls of fair access to and share of resources, with a reduced probability of survival as a consequence.

Discrimination may be extremely subtle, and surveys are often unable to capture inequality in resource allocation. Some of the factors most often mentioned include post-natal care, proper clothing, parental surveillance, breastfeeding, food allocation (both quantity and quality), recourse to health facilities (frequency and expenses), immunisation, etc. It is also expressed in other attitudes towards girls (such as with regards to schooling) that have no demographic consequences. All discrimination strategies towards girls do not invariably cause mortality, of course, as many Indian girls survive childhood in spite of severe deprivation. While it requires almost no financial or other parental effort, its own reliability as a way to eliminate daughters is limited. It may even be asked whether this constitutes a strategy per se, rather than merely being the random, unpredictable outcome of a certain set of practices.

Sex determination and selective abortion: Pre-natal diagnostic techniques involve two main technologies, viz. amniocentesis and ultrasonography. In India, pre-natal sex determination relies mostly on the latter, a non-invasive technology that is also easier and cheaper to conduct than amniocentesis, and is reliable after at least 14-16 weeks of gestation. Both of these techniques were first tested in India in 1974, starting with amniocentesis. By the 1980s, thousands of pre-natal clinics were already in operation.

Abortion in India benefited from an early liberal legislation – the MTP (Medical Termination of Pregnancy) Act, discussed since 1964, ratified in 1971 and introduced in 1974 (though not in Jammu & Kashmir). In 1975, the MTP Rules and Regulations defined when (12-20 weeks of pregnancy), by whom (registered allopathic doctors) and where unwanted pregnancies could be legally terminated. The Act was amended in 2002 and 2003, to improve women's access to safe abortion. One peculiar dimension of this Act is that it appears to focus on married women, and can be misconstrued as discriminating against single, divorced or widowed women. Apart from the usual social and health reasons, the most liberal provision of the Act includes contraceptive failure as a reason for abortion, paving the way for the probable use of abortion as a last-resort family-planning method.

The number of abortions that take place in India is poorly known, especially because many terminations take place outside registered centres and are performed by uncertified providers. Estimates vary from 13 to 21 per 1000 births, based on large-scale surveys and state statistics, while micro-level studies may provide lower estimates. In absolute terms, estimates are of 4-6 million abortions every year, but some figures go much higher. In the public health-care system, an abortion in 2006 could be obtained through 11,000 approved clinics, although with a disproportionate share of these being in urban areas. A large number of users in cities choose to go to private clinics, even if costs in public institutions are free or nominal. Only a small proportion of primary health centres provides MTP services.

Latest sex-selection technology: There are several sex-selection techniques not known to be widely available in India, even if the Ericsson method (of sperm sorting) may have been at some point available in clinics in Punjab.

Some of the characteristics of these techniques are worth mentioning. Two major pre-implantation methods exist that can be used for sex selection: sperm sorting (sperm that is sorted by sex and then used in artificial insemination or in-vitro fertilisation – IVF – procedures), and pre-implantation genetic diagnosis. These techniques, which are available in industrialised countries, are expensive and require well-equipped labs. For a variety of reasons, including cost and legal prohibition, these methods are not likely to be accessible to Indian residents in the near future. But to affluent Indians (who are able to travel or who have international connections), these methods may offer an almost undetectable way to carry out sex selection, without resorting to second-trimester abortion.

The technology of sex determination has also undergone constant progress since the introduction of amniocentesis and ultrasound. One of the latest products, of particular relevance to the Indian experience, is "foetal DNA testing". As the blood of the pregnant mother is known to contain the DNA of her baby after six weeks of gestation, a sample of this blood can be tested to identify the sex of the embryo. The test is reported to be 95 per cent accurate and costs less than US$ 300.

The potential of this technique for Indian users is enormous, especially given that testing can be done from a distance: simply send a sample by mail, and lab results are available a few days later through the Internet. Compared to classic scans, this method offers fast and early results with satisfactory reliability. Since the sex of the embryo can subsequently be determined about two months earlier than by ultrasound, this method offers to shorten the gestation period for aborting women. It may also prove more difficult to detect and monitor.

Knowledge and accessibility: The availability of sex-selection methods is first mediated by awareness of their existence. Traditional methods had long been in place in India, and were therefore well known in certain communities, with local specialists responsible for preserving the most sophisticated methods. New methods, such as sex-selective abortions, were unknown to most of India's population thirty years ago. Ever since, however, they have spread through multiple channels, ranging from interpersonal exchanges among users to aggressive publicity by suppliers. Because of the proximity of both ingredients of sex-selective abortions – sex identification and pregnancy termination – to family planning and reproductive-health efforts, these two procedures separately benefited from wide publicity, either as a component of modern pre-natal care or as part of fertility-control methods.

Amniocentesis and, later, ultrasound received wide publicity as modern instruments for the monitoring of the foetus, and to avoid birth defects. Initially, they were made available to pregnant mothers at a limited cost in well-equipped health centres. In many parts of India, recourse to multiple ultrasound examinations by expectant mothers is still extremely common, though rarely as an instrument to decide the fate of a pregnancy. Surveys have shown that knowledge of modern sex-selection instruments is today widespread, and that their diffusion most likely followed hierarchical channels, spreading from large cities to smaller towns to villages, and from more affluent groups towards the lower strata of local society.

Clinics: As pre-natal care was incorporated into India's reproductive-health efforts during this period, it received wide publicity as an essential tool to monitor the growth of the foetus. While sex determination was initially available through local government facilities, a change in health policy in the 1980s to regulate sex determination stimulated the growth of private-sector sex-selection services. Compared to government institutions, the private health sector offered services that were widespread, numerous and in several ways of better quality, even if less affordable. To many patients, the wide distribution of clinics around the country meant that the necessary equipment to perform sex determination was available in almost all localities.

While considered expensive at the beginning, scanning later benefited from rapidly decreasing costs, largely fuelled by competition as the private health sector developed. Ultrasound is today a relatively easy technique to implement. It does not require a highly trained staff or extra operational expenditure. A machine costs around Rs 500,000 (about US$ 11,600), and individual ultrasound test cost Rs 300-1000. After the amendment of the PC & PNDT (Pre-conception and Pre-natal Diagnostic Techniques) Act in 2003, the total number of registered units two years later was 26,954. Enterprising doctors and clinic managers have played an active role in the diffusion of sex-selection technology, along with health workers who have publicised the services.

Providers acted mostly as advisers to women who wanted to avoid births, while the fact that, in many cases, the births to be avoided happened to be female births was considered irrelevant, at least initially. Familiar with both technologies and their practicalities, health workers and doctors at various levels were thus the first channels for quality information on the feasibility of sex-selective abortions. Today, physicians are largely conscious of the potential perverse effects of this technology, and are opposed to sex selection and its ethical implications.

As early as 1986, the Federation of Obstetric and Gynaecological Societies of India passed a resolution against pre-natal sex determination and sex-selective abortions. Since then, many medical practitioners have joined campaigns against the misuse of these technologies, with the support of professional associations. In 2006, the Indian Medical Association took a firm stand against sex selection, and intends to collaborate fully with the implementation of the PC & PNDT Act. Doctors have, however, been put in a difficult position due to the activities of a small number among them – those who became rich by performing illegal sex diagnoses or sex-selective abortions. Initially, during surveys in the 1980s, many doctors freely acknowledged their role in offering sexselection services; ever since then, however, they have been more careful in their public declarations.

It should also be noted that it is the medical community that often voices the most favourable comments regarding sex selection, including criticism over the legal provisions of the PC & PNDT Act. In particular, some doctors have stressed that sex selection, despite being condemnable, exists only in response to latent demands from women and their families, and therefore is merely fulfilling a need. Many other arguments have also been advanced in favour of sex selection: the freedom and autonomy of patients to decide upon such procedures for themselves, the family-planning aspect of avoiding unwanted births through abortion, deterrence vis-à-vis infanticide, humanitarian attempts to "relieve" women and girl children of their social and economic burdens, etc.

Legislation: Legislation is now a central part of the supply framework for sex-selection in India. The major change related to supply in recent years actually relates to the effect of successive legislations, geared towards preventing the misuse of ultrasound technology to detect the sex of a foetus; and, to a far lesser extent, to the stricter implementation of existing criminal laws against infanticide in some areas. In the eyes of potential users of sex-selection methods, law enforcement has meant increasing difficulties in getting access to new technology and providers, as well as increased monitoring of their equipment and activities.

As a result, access to these facilities has become more difficult of late, as well as more expensive. Many providers have been obliged to stop providing information on a foetus's sex to new customers, while illegal abortions are increasingly conducted by untrained and unregistered practitioners, with serious potential health consequences for women.

Social acceptability of sex-selection: Sex-selection needs to be acceptable and conceivable in both principle and procedure. There are very few known philosophical or religious principles that bar individuals or groups in India from envisaging a deliberate choice in the sex composition of their offspring. Some limited sections of the population may be opposed to sex discrimination on a larger plane, but when confronted with individual choices and facing certain constraints, general principles of gender equity may carry little weight. Another factor related to the legitimacy of sex selection may also be the acceptability of using rational reasoning to make a decision about one's offspring. To a large extent, rapid fertility decline itself has shown that people have accepted the principle of controlled fertility, and it may therefore logically follow that manipulating the "contents" of one's fertility is part of this fundamental behavioural change.

A more significant dimension relates to the actual methods used, such as the difference between infanticide and abortion: the latter option is far less repugnant to most Indians, even though in some isolated villages or communities, sex-selective infanticide has been condoned in the relatively recent past. While perceived as progress in moral terms, abortion still remains a very sensitive matter for many mothers. It often goes unreported in surveys, and it is usually carried out on the sly. In some specific religious communities – such as among Christians and Muslims – abortion is condemned, and sex ratios are at near-normal levels.

Economic rationale: A common explanation for gender discrimination usually boils down to the fact that girls constitute a source of impoverishment for their family. It is therefore appealing to attempt a cost-benefit analysis, in order to examine specific "costs" related to girls, as well as "benefits" accruing from boys. It is important to emphasise at the outset that this overview is unavoidably based on "stylised" facts, which may not always fit nicely with the anthropological diversity of India, where marriage and kinship systems are extremely heterogeneous. Readers familiar with this diversity will therefore have to endure what may appear to be generalisations concealing significant exceptions or anomalies.

Cost factors: According to many Indian parents, raising a girl entails extra costs related to protective efforts extended especially to daughters. Girls are perceived to be particularly vulnerable, as family honour seems, at times, to rest exclusively on women's behaviour, rather than on men's. But apart from this aspect, raising daughters cannot be said to be more expensive than raising sons, especially when they receive care and education of inferior quality compared to their brothers. As such, it is only with reference to costs arising during or after their marriage that daughters appear to be more "expensive" than sons. In addition, though the "investment" in daughters is essentially the same as sons before marriage, this money is subsequently considered wasted due to the "patrilocal" nature of marriage, meaning that married couples in India generally live near the husband's family, rather than the wife's.

Marriage and related expenditures constitute a large category of costs. This includes several sub-categories, such as wedding expenses borne by the bride's family, customary gifts to the groom's side, and especially dowry, or even post-marriage expenses. Dowry encompasses cash, gold and other jewellery, and additional durables, and it constitutes the major bulk of marriage expenses, often exceeding several years' of household income. Indeed, it has been observed that a dowry's amount is more proportional to the "quality" of the groom and his family – education, background, income, etc. – than to the potential share for the bride herself in the family assets. High dowry will ensure a proper marriage into the best possible family – hypergamy being a tacit norm – and ensures additional prestige and reputation to the bride's family. It is important to stress that the very low status customarily assigned to unmarried daughters in India usually prevents them from opting out of the system by remaining single.

Dowry arrangements have long been common among higher-status groups in North India, but since Independence such arrangements have recorded a formidable spread towards both lower castes and South India. There are today very few communities in which dowry has not been introduced. Another contemporary feature of the dowry system relates to its apparent unending inflation, fuelled by the combined effect of enhanced competition for suitable grooms, growing economic heterogeneity within endogamous caste groups, affluence in time of rapid economic growth and increasing materialism. The resource flow is almost the opposite in the case of boys, as the groom's family will directly receive a large part of the dowry from the bride's family. For that reason, raising and educating boys seem highly profitable, whereas girls could be seen to mean further expenses.

A traditional nickname for a woman within her family is *paraya dhan*, which means "somebody else's property". Indeed, the traditional Hindu ideal of "giving away" one's daughters (*kanyadana*) has become economic nonsense. In rural settings, rich peasants – among whom women generally enjoy no secure rights over family land, as daughters or as widows – may have to part with some of their fields in order to cover dowry expenditures. But among the lower classes, the picture is slightly different, owing to the absence of transmissible assets. As such, the women's labour is considered a more decisive contribution to the prosperity of the household. While dowry has been introduced into many poor communities, such as the landless, the amounts transacted have remained moderate, including for poor families.

Economic support and other benefits: In settings characterised by joint family arrangements, resources are usually pooled between parents and children. This is the case for a large part of the dowry transfer, which may not directly reach the newly wed couple. But the later income of married children will also benefit their parents, as is the case of rural households in which sons work on family land or business. Joint family cohabitation also means that parents can enjoy constant financial and emotional support from their sons' families, whereas married daughters are not supposed to contribute to their parents' expenses after marriage. This is also true for married sons who are not living with their parents, as they are expected to contribute to their parents' well being until the end of their lives.

In a country where pension benefits and social security are almost entirely absent, long-time support extended by sons is a major source of security for ageing parents. But this may not be true to the same degree everywhere in India, as some communities or social categories have a more balanced and less patrilineal family structure.

Symbols and tradition: A comprehensive cost-benefit analysis of children distinguished by sex also needs to be extended to non-financial domains. For instance, sons living in the vicinity represent a source of protection and affection for their parents. In many marriage systems, daughters are supposed to live away from their parents, and therefore have limited interaction with them after marriage.There are many other more-symbolic advantages in having sons. First of all, as in any patrilineal society, sons are vital to continue the family lineage (*gotra*), and often the family activities. Since daughters are usually excluded from an equal share of the inheritance, surviving boys are assured to inherit their parents' property, and will carry on the family name.

In fact, in the most common exogamous system in India (in which grooms marry same-caste brides, but from different lineages and localities), women join the *gotra* of their husband at marriage, thereby losing membership in their original lineage. Sons are subsequently the only legitimate descendants in this patriarchal system, as their married sisters belong to another lineage altogether.

One of the most publicised roles for Hindu sons is also to perform the requisite rituals upon the death of their father, a task from which women are customarily excluded. The prominent role of sons within the patrilineal system has, of course, added prestige to their status, and is a common source of pride for parents. Many dimensions covered in this section relate to status symbols and to purely economic advantages. For that reason, it is fair to say that high-ranking communities and high-income groups will be especially responsive to demands related to ritual, reputation and financial exchange. Lower-status or lower-income groups, such as backward castes or tribal populations, are therefore in a different position, and son preference in these communities is usually less acute than in the rest of society. But the powerful top-down mechanisms at work in contemporary India mean that many high-caste or urban customs are being "borrowed" by other classes and communities, in a bid to improve their overall social status.

3

Rural Women and Education

The past three decades have witnessed a steadily increasing awareness of the need to empower women through measures to increase social, economic and political equity, and broader access to fundamental human rights, improvements in nutrition, basic health and education. Along with awareness of the subordinate status of women has come the concept of gender as an overarching socio-cultural variable, seen in relation to other factors, such as race, class, age and ethnicity. Gender is not synonymous with women, nor is it a zero-sum game implying loss for men; rather, it refers to both women and men, and to their status, relative to each other. Gender equality refers to that stage of human social development at which "the rights, responsibilities and opportunities of individuals will not be determined by the fact of being born male or female," in other words, a stage when both men and women realise their full potential.

Women constitute half of the country's population accounting for 495.7 million as per the 2001 census and represent 48.3 per cent of the population. As a result of the space created for women in the local governance structures with the 73rd and 74th Amendments nearly a million women have gained entry at different levels of the grassroots governance body—the panchayat.

The policy of reservation of one-third seats for women in these village level panchayats and urban municipalities, has enabled women to hold elected positions in the three tiers of the panchayati raj institutions (PRIs)—the gram panchayat, panchayat samiti and the Zilla Parishad (at the district HQs). In keeping with the frequently changing paradigms for social development, that is laying greater stress on gender issues at the global and national level now, moving towards more gender equality is a part of the process of governance in the country. Empowerment and development are two sides of the same coin.

The basic objective of development, as defined in the Human Development Report is to enlarge people's choices. It is based on three key components:

— Equality of opportunity for all people in society;
— Sustainability of such opportunity from one generation to the next.
— Empowerment of the people so that they participate in, and benefit from, the development process.

These components have many dimensions. They can be articulated as:

— Equal access to basic social services, including education and health;
— Equal opportunity for participating in political and economic decision-making;
— Equal reward for equal work;
— Equal protection under the law;
— Elimination of discrimination by gender and violence against women;

— Equal rights of citizens in all areas of life, both public—as in workplace—and private—as in the homes. And so on.

For too long it was assumed that as the development process unfolded, benefits would trickle down to all income groups. It was also considered as being gender neutral. But, experience has shown otherwise. Moving towards gender equality is now seen as a political process that calls for a new way of thinking, in which the stereotyping of women and men gives way to the philosophy that all people are essential agents of change.

Investing in women's capabilities and empowering them to exercise choices contributes to economic growth and the overall development in the country.

As a result, the importance of investing in women has gown steadily in every successive five-year-plans of the country. In fact, women form a separate category for planning interventions as they have a direct bearing upon the country's total development. Women who represent 90 per cent in the informal sector have been the backbone of the rural economy, but unfortunately their contribution to the development process has remained invisible.

They are, actually being hit the hardest in the wake of the changing development paradigms, especially of economic liberalisation and globalisation apart from suffering of social backwardness. It is therefore that these women are given priority, requiring special attention in several government programming.

Reviewing the opportunities for women in education, the National Census data shows that some gains have been made in this sphere. In fact the female literacy rate went up from 12.95 per cent in 1961 to 54.16 per cent in 2001. It grew twice the rate than that for males during the same period. In the past decade, the number of absolute female illiterates has also come down indicating that the adult literacy initiatives have made a difference. Also, the gap between the female and male illiterates and dropouts has started narrowing down.

However, the progress is not uniform in the country. There are not only inter-state variations but also intra-state differences. Around 300 districts have lower literacy levels than the national average. Kerala recorded the highest literacy rate of 87.86 per cent for females while Bihar recorded the lowest at 33.57 per cent.

When looking at the higher education figures, though there has been a substantial increase in the enrolment for higher education between 1996/97 to 1999/2000, it is the technical education like engineering or architecture that has doubled from 0.49 in 1996/97 to 0.80 in 1999/2000. In contrast, enrolment for Graduate courses has gone up from 18.20 lakhs to 26.62 lakhs. In medicine, in the corresponding years female enrolment also went up from 14.9 lakhs to 22.0 lakhs. Looking at the divide between rural and urban, it is the rural areas that have recorded a quantum jump in higher education than the urban areas.

The female work participation rate also registered an increase from 14.2 per cent in 1971 to 22.27 in 1991. But it is still much lower than male participation in both urban and rural areas. In next decade it may record a decline as the total work participation has shown a downward trend.

Women's share in the organised sector has also gone up in the past two decades from 11 per cent to 17.2 per cent. The same is the case of their employment in the public sector from 8 per cent to 14.5 per cent. It is expected to go up further as more and more service sector jobs move into India globally. While representation of women in the administration (government service) increased marginally, their role in the decision-making levels through all the competitive services accounted for only 7.6 per cent in 2000.

The above data indicates that though opportunities and choices are gradually expanding for women, the pyramid gets narrow at the top making it far more difficult for them to get to the top positions. It is a universal phenomenon and not limited to India alone.

Rural areas in contrast have a different story to tell. There has been a definite impact on the participation of women in decision-making positions via the panchayati raj institutions. The re-vitalisation of the panchayat system has become the route for women to participate and leave their mark on the functioning of the grassroots democracy.

Out of 475 Zilla Parishads (District bodies) in the country 158 are chaired by women. At the block level out of 51,000 members of block samitis 17,000 are women. Nearly one-third of the mayors of the municipalities are women. In the recent PRI elections many women were contesting and had won in addition to the reserved seats for women candidates in the open general pool, competing with male candidates. In Karnataka, Kerala and West Bengal they had won 43.45 per cent, 36.4 per cent and 35.4 per cent of seats respectively. However, the all India figure showed that there was a decline of 9 per cent between 1995 to 2001.

Moving from the grassroots to the top of the governance ladder, the number of women in parliament has gone up from 37 (5.2 per cent) in 1952 to 70 (8.5 per cent) in 2001. It has taken almost fifty years to double yet it continues to be low.

Empowered women socially, economically and politically would add to economic growth and overall development this would in turn bring in more women into the fold of better opportunities and more choices. The process is on, but the pace may differ from state to state.

GENDER GAPS IN EDUCATION

Educational attainment is, without doubt, the most fundamental prerequisite for empowering women in all spheres of society, for without education of comparable quality and content to that given to boys and men, and relevant to existing knowledge and real needs, women are unable to access well-paid, formal sector jobs, advance within them, participate in, and be represented in government and gain political influence.

Moreover, the risk increases for society as a whole that the next generation of children will be similarly ill-prepared. If, as a broad body of empirical work has shown, education and literacy reduce mortality rates of children-including the bias toward female child mortality-and help reduce fertility rates,the importance of literacy for women is all the greater, considering that women still constitute two-thirds of the world's illiterate population.

In addition, the number of women represented among tertiary level educators is lower than among primary level educators. However, if the content of the educational curriculum and the attitudes of teachers serve merely to reinforce prevalent stereotypes and injustices, then the mere fact of literacy and education does not, in and of itself, close the gender gap; schooling as a catalyst for change in gender relations will be more effective only if appropriate attention is also given to curriculum content and the retraining of those who deliver it.

Information and communication technologies, which have become a potent driving force of the development process, represent yet another dimension in which a knowledge gap has emerged between women and men: a gender-based digital divide. A study by the USAID has found that countless women in the developing world are further removed from the information age because of their lower levels of education and deeply ingrained negative attitudes towards other forms of achievement. "Without access to information technology, an understanding of its significance and the ability to use it for social and economic gain, women in the developing world will be further marginalised from the mainstream of their communities, their countries and the world."

WOMEN'S EDUCATION POLICIES AND PROGRAMMES

In India, women and girls receive far less education than men, due both to social norms and fears of violence. The country has the largest population of non-school-going working girls. India's constitution guarantees free primary school education for both boys and girls up to age 14. This goal has been repeatedly reconfirmed, but primary education in India is not universal. Overall, the literacy rate for women is 54.16 per cent versus 65.38 per cent for men, according to the census report 2001.

Eradication of female illiteracy has been one of the major concerns of the government of India since independence. The government and non-governmental organisations have established a number of initiatives for the educational development of women and girls. India is rich in policies, thus almost every conceivable strategy to promote girls' education has been covered. The problem lies in implementation. It is therefore necessary to concentrate on making the system work and deliver the services.

The Indian government has taken certain steps to promote women's status and overcome the problems they face in society. The education ministry has both formal and informal education programmes for girls, the latter in collaboration with NGOs. The Department of Women and Child Development formulates strategies, policies, and programmes, enacts or amends legislation, and guides and supports work done by other government or nongovernmental bodies for improving the status of women and children. The department has initiated training programmes for employment, awareness building, and gender sensitisation. It has also established hostels for working women. The impact of such initiatives is not known because of the lack of documentation.

An important education policy from a women's perspective has been instituted in the state of Andhra Pradesh where one-third of all places in institutes for higher education are reserved for women. It is possible that such a policy may increase the number of women who opt to study ICTs and related fields at higher levels of education.

The Fourth World Conference on Women, Beijing 1995, reaffirmed the commitments made by governments and called upon the international community to intensify efforts. Four important world conferences, one after another, bombarded the world with messages of equality, empowerment, human rights and universal access to the tools of knowledge – i.e. education. While cynics in all societies may brush aside the impact of such international agreements, it is widely acknowledged that, as a result of intensive advocacy, girls' and women's education has been accepted as a developmental priority. Availability of international development assistance for basic education and women's education (especially in India) has gone up significantly.

More importantly, there has been a noticeable change in Government and donor perceptions of gender issues in education and the importance of reaching out to girls in order to achieve the goal of universal elementary education. Successive Human Development Reports brought out by the United Nations forced political leaders and administrators to acknowledge the inherent value of education in building capabilities of people to survive with dignity. Donors supporting education programmes in the developing world flagged the gender agenda. This environment coupled with the realisation of the importance of sustained advocacy resulted in a virtual explosion of data, case studies, reports and conferences on girls' and women's education. The popular media has also started paying some attention to glaring gender disparities in educational access and achievement. All these contributed in no small measure to creating an environment for introspection and change.

The climate is right to pool all the energies and push hard to ensure that policy level commitment of the Government is translated into action – i.e. bridging the gap between intention and action. We are at a very critical juncture in India. We are at a point when sustained pressure to ensure universal access to and retention in schools and enhancing the quality and content of education at all levels may actually bear fruit. A well known educationist commented that even in a very gender iniquitous society like Rajasthan families no longer need to be convinced of the importance of sending their girls to school. Wherever accessible and good quality educational facilities are provided, girls come in large numbers.

The inherent social bias against women in rural areas manifests in different forms. Early school dropout is one major problem young female students face in rural areas. Rural women education efforts will be significantly enhanced if the female student dropout in secondary/ high schools in rural areas could be reduced. The important thing to note is that, these young female students already have the basic education at the primary level, have the ability to read, write and communicate with others and are in a situation where higher education would significantly enhance their knowledge horizons. Losing a female student through dropout is similar to losing an existing and valuable customer and any business literature would attest to the need to retain such customers. Thus retaining female students in rural schools becomes paramount.

It is well recognised that there are socioeconomic and family reasons which result in female student dropout in rural schools and IT, as a tool, cannot address these issues. Our strategy is to use IT as a information tool and IT training and its attendant job potential as a socioeconomic incentive to retain students in schools. It is worth noting that this model would be equally applicable to socially disadvantaged female students studying in poorly funded schools in large cities.

Despite good intentions and national strategies to combat this problem, many governments in highly populated countries such as India are unable to meet this challenge because of the exploding population, limited resources and competing demands from other sectors. The economic and social disparities between cities and rural areas also result in quality educational and social infrastructure being located in metropolitan cities, making it inaccessible to people located in smaller towns and villages as well as to those in the lower socioeconomic strata.

Usually, the inhabitants of remote villages and other rural areas are forced to travel great distances to access such facilities. This is an issue in many parts of the world, particularly where the population is spread out over large areas and the infrastructure is unevenly distributed. In India however, with over one billion people, the problem tends to be much more visible when compared to other countries.

Seethalakshmi Ramaswamy College for women is a charitable, non-profit educational institution and its educational programmes have national accreditation from NAAC (National Assessment and Accreditation Council). NAAC is the apex body in India that certifies educational programmes. The college is also recognised by the Ford Foundation. Located in one of the smaller cities of Tamil Nadu, this long standing educational institution has substantial track record in socially oriented programmes in rural areas surrounding Tiruchirapalli. Founded for the very purpose of the uplift of women in post independence India, this institution has maintained the service ethos to the present day and has won many laurels in the community. The existing infrastructure, the service ethos and current outreach programmes that target rural women ensure that the proposed project will have long term sustainability.

HIGHER EDUCATION FOR RURAL WOMEN

Women at large and rural women in particular work at a variety of tasks. They have little time for leisure but what is shameful is that they have little or no control over the productive resources. The challenge of providing higher education to rural Indian women must be put in the context of the demographics and cultural traditions of the country. While great efforts have been made at population control resulting in a rate of population increase of just 1.8 per cent per year, in a country of 1 billion people, that still means an annual population increase of some 18 million people who require all the essentials of life as well as education at all levels. The population increase in and of itself presents a staggering educational and financial challenge.

Education will be used as an agent of basic change in the status of women. In order to neutralise the accumulated distortions of the past, there will be a well-conceived edge in favour of women. The National Education System will play a positive, interventionist role in the empowerment of women. It will foster the development of new values through redesigned curricula, textbooks, the training and orientation of teachers, decision-makers and administrators, and the active involvement of educational institutions. This will be an act of faith and social engineering. Women's Studies will be an act of faith and social engineering. Women's studies will be promoted as a part of various courses and educational institutions encouraged to take up active programmes to further women's development.

The removal of women's illiteracy and obstacles inhibiting their access to and retention in elementary education will receive overriding priority, through provision of special support services, setting of time targets, and effective monitoring. Major emphasis will be laid on women's participation in vocational, technical and professional education at different levels. The policy of nondiscrimination will be pursued vigorously to eliminate sex stereotyping in vocational and professional courses and to promote women's participation in non-traditional occupations, as well as in existing and emergent technologies.

The primary emphasis is on organising women at the grassroots, to encourage reflection, self-reliance and collective learning and productive activity. This link between grassroot organisation—of women producers, and their empowerment to participate more effectively in the developmental and the political process by giving them 'social strength' is also admitted in the Seventh Five Year Plan and in some plan programmes adopted by different ministries.

There is nothing new in this idea. It has been debated and articulated in virtually all conferences on women and development, national and international. What is new is the effort to enlist the active support of educational institutions in bringing this about. Till recently, all concerned with planning strategies to bring about gender equality—at national and international levels tended to depend on government action or action by non-governmental organisations. The support of individual academics was harnessed mainly to do research—diagnostic or evaluative. The first suggestion that educational institutions also need to play a role in this field was hinted at the Copenhagen Conference, but the Programme of Action does not clearly articulate how that role should be played.

In the case of developing countries particularly, intervention for women's equality and development, whether prompted by government or other agencies, always has to contain a hard core of educational, information gathering, communicational and training activities. It is impracticable to expect bureaucracy to play this role. NGOs concerned with women's issues in these countries are mostly based in urban areas, and lack both human and financial resources to undertake all the tasks that are involved—research, communication, mobilisation, training, obtaining resource support, even legal and political support in some cases. Nor do many such organisations exist in all developing countries. But educational institutions, of varied quality, have come to exist in most parts of the developing world. They do possess some of the skills, the infrastructural support, and above all the human resources to play this role.

If education is to become an active agent for ending gender inequality, it requires a new perspective, new methods and tools, and new knowledge—(a) about the centrality of women's role to correct the peasant iniquitous and destructive path of development; and (b) about the origin of women's subordination in society. It is the contention of this chapter that the key to these two critical issues lie in the past and contemporary histories of rural women, to a far greater extent than in the experiences of their counterparts in urban areas, because one finds far clearer gender differentials in the assessment of problems, priorities, values and demands in rural than in urban areas in developing countries.

The problem of invisibility, undercounting and undervaluation of women's work in agriculture surfaced with a vengeance during the women's decade, not only due to the pressure of feminist scholarship, but the growing developmental crisis, especially in food production, environmental destruction with deforestation, the 'other' energy crisis, and mass migration of the rural unemployed to cities and metropolitan countries in search of employment. This forced various international and national agencies to revise their earlier estimates of women's contribution to agriculture.

Swaminathan argues that ignoring rural women's higher skills in certain agricultural operations, such as seed selection, storage, pre-germination tests, pollination, transplantation, all post-harvest operations, as well as cattle care and other livestock rearing has, in fact, arrested the growth of agricultural productivity. Improving their access to available new knowledge, not only in these areas, but in soil fertility and fertiliser management, integrated post and weed management, water and soil conservation, would make a major impact on rice agriculture.

A great deal of evidence is now available that links the present food crisis in Africa to the neglect of the subsistence sector, where women predominate, in African agricultural development. Women are the 'prime-movers' in the food economy, but have been losing ground steadily in access to quality land, better implements and seeds, and loss of customary usufructory rights to land, irrespective of their marital status. As in the case of poor rural women in Asia, their labour time has increased, but the rewards are less.

Despite legislative protection of equal pay for equal work in many countries, all over the world rural women receive less wages for their labour. This is acknowledged in the World Labour Report, but is inadequately documented. One major problem that has affected both planners' and analysts of rural society, is the myth of the homogeneity of rural women. Rural societies like urban societies in most parts of the world, are fragmented by socio-economic class, occupational groups, and ethnic and other cultural identities. Except in occasional isolated areas where simple communities still continue to subsist on primitive agriculture or food gathering, most rural communities have experienced radical changes in their socio-economic organisation, production systems and relations, and the changes that come with increasing penetration of a magnetised economy, state and legal control over basic resources and population pressures. Different groups of rural women are affected differently by these changes. In the South Asian context, a hierarchical pattern of social organisation had emerged much earlier than elsewhere. In such societies, withdrawal of women from visible economic activity was, and continues to be a symbol of higher social status.

IMPROVING THE STATUS OF WOMEN AND EDUCATIONAL ATTAINMENT: A STUDY IN KERALA

An important policy prescription for improving the status of women in India is to improve their educational attainment. Human capital theory suggests that education and training are significant determinants of employment and earnings. Therefore, it is desirable that Indian women acquire the necessary skills that would enhance their employment and earnings capacity in the labour market as well as improving their status within the household.

While the overall literacy rate and educational attainment among Indian women are low compared to those of developed countries, there have been substantial improvements in the human capital attainment of Indian women over the past few years. Yet women in India are still confined to casual labour or marginal work at home or in the field, while men occupy more lucrative jobs. Educated unemployment is widely prevalent among both men and women in India. This is especially puzzling when we focus on the state of Kerala. Kerala ranks first among Indian states in women's literacy rates and in both Human Development and Gender Development Index. Yet the unemployment rate among both men and women in Kerala is very high, and educated unemployment is widely prevalent.

Recently, there has been growing discomfort with the concept of the "Kerala model," partly due to the anomalous relationship between high educational attainment and low labour force participation of Kerala women in the labour market. The objective of this study is to probe into this paradox in order to have a better understanding of the relationship between education and employment in the context of the state of Kerala. It is not enough to focus on literacy and employment without probing into the nature of human capital investment made by women in Kerala as well as the specific skills that are demanded by employers in the labour market. At the same time, the social and cultural environment of this particular state also needs to be studied in order to understand the nature of gender relations and the subsequent effects in educational attainment and labour market status of women.

Ideally, the macro data provided by Census of India and the National Sample Survey Organisation (NSSO) that will be the primary focus of this study should be augmented with detailed micro-level data in order to explain this apparent paradox in Kerala. Unfortunately, such micro-level data are extremely sparse. Table 3.1 shows the female literacy rate in India as reported by the 2001 census. While the overall female literacy rate in India is 54.16 per cent, the different states and union territories exhibit significant differences in female literacy rates. The state of Bihar ranks the lowest while Kerala ranks the highest in female literacy rates in the country.

Table 3.1. State-wise percentage of female literacy in the country as per 2001 Census

Sl.No.	*Name of the State*	*Percentage of Female Literacy*
1.	Andhra Pradesh	51.17
2.	Arunachal Pradesh	44.24
3.	Assam	56.03
4.	Bihar	33.57
5.	Chattisgarh	52.40
6.	Delhi	75.00
7.	Goa	75.51
8.	Gujarat	58.60
9.	Haryana	56.31
10.	Himachal Pradesh	68.08
11.	Jammu & Kashmir	41.82
12.	Jharkhand	39.38
13.	Karnataka	57.45
14.	Kerala	87.86
15.	Madhya Pradesh	50.28
16.	Maharashtra	67.51
17.	Manipur	59.70
18.	Meghlaya	60.41
19.	Mizoram	86.13
20.	Nagaland	61.92
21.	Orissa	50.97
22.	Punjab	63.55
23.	Rajasthan	44.34
24.	Sikkim	61.46
25.	Tamil Nadu	64.55
26.	Tripura	65.41
27.	Uttaranchal	60.26
28.	Uttar Pradesh	42.98
29.	West Bengal	60.22

	Union Territories	
1.	Andaman & Nicobar Islands	75.29
2.	Chandigarh	76.65
3.	Dadra & Nagar Haveli	42.99
4.	Daman & Diu	70.37
5.	Lakshadweep	81.56
6.	Pondicherry	74.16
	All India	**54.16**

Table 3.2 shows the 2001 census data on male and female literacy rates and the gender gap in literacy across all the districts in Kerala. While the overall literacy rate for both males and females is uniformly high compared with the states in India, the districts of Kannur, Thrissur, Ernakulam, Idukki, Kottayam, Alappuzha, and Pathanamthitta exhibit some of the highest female literacy rates in the state of Kerala.

Table 3.2. 2001 census data on male and female literacy rates

State	*Female Literacy, 2001*	*Male Literacy, 2001*
Kerala	88%	94%
Mizoram	86%	91%
Lakshadweep	82%	93%
All India average	54%	76%
Rajasthan	44.3%	76.5%
Arunachal Pradesh	44.2%	64%
Uttar Pradesh	43%	70%
Jammu & Kashmir	42%	66%
Jharkhand	40%	68%
Bihar	33.6%	60.3%

What is particularly interesting is that while the overall rural female literacy rate in India is 46.58 per cent (Census of India 2001), the female literacy rate in rural Kerala exceeds 90 per cent in the above districts. This makes Kerala an outlier among all Indian states. The gender disparity in literacy rate in Kerala is negligible compared with other Indian states. The gender gap in literacy in Kerala is highest in the district of Kasaragod, while the rate is lowest in the districts of Kottayam and Pathanamthitta.

Table 3.3 shows the level of educational attainment for both males and females in Kerala. The table shows that the gender disparity in education at every stage is very low.

From the beginning of the century, female educational attainment in the state has been very high as the government of Kerala placed high priority on educational spending. Literacy was much higher than anywhere in India as early as the eighteenth century. The state of Kerala spends more on education at every level compared with India in general, with the highest percentage allocated for elementary education and the lowest for technical education.

Overall, in India, 88 per cent of women in higher education are confined to majors in arts and commerce, while only 1 per cent of women choose occupations such as engineering. Women choose low-paying occupations such as school teachers, nurses, clerks, and typists. From the limited data that we could find, it seems that the majority of females in Kerala are confined to low-paying occupations such as clerks, nurses, and teachers.

It is surprising that women in Kerala continue to choose traditional female occupations that are mostly low paying, in light of the fact that Kerala ranks first among Indian states in Human Development and Gender Development Index. Women in Kerala have always enjoyed a better status in society than their female counterparts in the rest of India. While a male child is typically considered to be more valuable than a female child in India, the sex ratio (females/1000 males) in Kerala shows (table 3.2) a different scenario. Except for

Table 3.3. Literacy, Gender Gap and Gender Gap adjusted Literacy Rates in Indian States during 1991-2001

States	1991					1995					2001				
	M	*F*	*T*	*GG*	*AdjT*	*M*	*F*	*T*	*GG*	*AdjT*	*M*	*F*	*T*	*GG*	*AdjT*
Andhra Pr.	55	33	44	22	26	60	37	49	23	30	71	51	61	20	44
Bihar	52	23	38	29	17	59	28	44	31	21	64	37	51	27	29
Delhi	82	67	75	15	61	86	74	80	12	69	87	75	82	12	71
Gujarat	73	49	61	24	41	77	50	64	27	42	81	59	70	22	51
Haryana	69	40	56	29	32	72	52	63	20	46	79	56	69	23	49
Himachal Pr.	75	52	64	23	44	81	61	71	20	53	86	68	77	18	61
Karnataka	67	44	56	23	37	67	51	59	16	45	76	57	67	19	50
Kerala	94	86	90	8	82	95	89	91	6	85	94	88	91	6	85
Madhya Pr.	58	29	44	29	22	61	34	48	27	27	77	51	64	26	42
Maharashtra	77	52	65	25	44	83	62	73	21	55	86	68	77	18	61
Orissa	63	35	49	28	27	66	42	54	24	34	76	51	64	25	43
Punjab	66	50	59	16	45	68	54	62	14	49	76	64	70	12	59
Rajasthan	55	20	39	35	14	59	26	43	33	19	76	44	61	32	35
Tamil Nadu	74	51	63	23	43	76	54	65	22	46	82	65	73	17	58
Uttar Pr.	56	25	42	31	19	63	34	49	29	26	75	50	60	25	40
West Bengal	68	47	58	21	40	76	55	66	21	48	78	60	69	18	53
INDIA	64	39	52	25	32	69	46	58	23	39	76	54	65	22	46
Coeff of Variation	16.3	37.7	23.9	27.4	45.5	14.6	32.5	21.2	32.1	39.2	8.7	20.5	13.5	31.7	26.2

Note: M- Male, F- Female, T- Total, GG- Gender Gap, Adj T- GG adjusted Total.

the districts of Wayanad and ldukki, the ratio of females to males in all the districts of Kerala exceeds 1000.

What is remarkable is that this pattern is consistent in both rural and urban areas. The corresponding national sex ratio in India as reported in Census 2001 is 933. Ever since censuses have been conducted in India, Kerala women have outnumbered men. The pride and independence among the matrilineal women of Kerala has instilled in them the desire to achieve high literacy and educational attainment. It is natural that educated women in Kerala prefer to be employed in the skilled white-collar sector of the labour market.

Unemployment among Educated Males and Females

There exists chronic unemployment among the educated females in Kerala. The unemployment rate of the educated labour force in Kerala and in India during 1983 and 1987-88. The data come from the National Sample Survey Organisation (NSSO), which categorises "Usual Principal Status" as being in the labour force for more than six months preceding the date of survey. During 1987-88, urban unemployment among females who had a college degree was 19.6 per cent while the unemployment rate among females with a secondary education was 52.7 per cent.

The corresponding rates for men were 7.3 per cent and 23.6 per cent, respectively. The unemployment rate among females in rural areas is much higher than the unemployment rate in urban areas and indicates even fewer opportunities for women. During 1987-88, rural unemployment among female graduates was 45 per cent while the unemployment rate among females with a secondary education was 60 per cent. The higher unemployment rate among educated rural women can partly be attributed to the unavailability of skilled white-collar jobs that are predominantly located in urban areas.

The female work participation rate is lowest in the districts of Malappuram and Kozhikode, while it is relatively higher in the districts of Wayand, Kasaragod, Palakkad, Idukki, Ernakulam, and Alappuzha. The work participation rate among females is typically higher in rural areas where more jobs are available in the agricultural sector. Unfortunately, in the absence of detailed data about the employment sectors in each district, occupational details, and worker characteristics, we cannot speculate much as to why such variations exist among the different districts of Kerala.

Employment Patterns among Women in Kerala

In Kerala, there are different types of employment into three categories: the primary sector, the secondary sector, and the tertiary sector. The primary sector consists of occupations such as cultivators and agricultural labourers and comprises mostly unskilled workers. A person is categorised as a cultivator if he or she is employed in cultivation of land owned by government or other institutions. The cultivator pays the government, institutions, and individuals back in cash or in-kind for use of their land. On the other hand, an agricultural worker works on someone else's land in return for wages or in-kind payments.

The secondary sector includes construction and manufacturing jobs as well as household industry workers. If one or more members of the household participate in the production, servicing, making, or selling of goods, they are categorised as being employed in household industries. The tertiary sector includes jobs in the service sector and public sector jobs.

The sectoral distribution of the female work force in Kerala is significantly different from that of India. While the primary sector still remains the largest source of employment for both men and women in India, not even half the work force in Kerala is employed in the primary sector.

Women in Kerala are also overrepresented in the secondary sector compared with the overall distribution of female employment in this sector in India. In 1991, about 21.65 per cent of women in Kerala were employed in the secondary sector whereas the corresponding female employment rate in this sector in India was only 8.07 per cent. Employment in non-household manufacturing increased from 12.47 per cent to 14.8 per cent during 1981-91, while female employment in household industry declined from 7.64 per cent to 5.93 per cent during the same period. The decline in many household industries in Kerala such as cashew and beedi, which primarily employ women, perhaps explains the decline in female employment in this sector.

In 1991, 29.74 per cent of Kerala women were employed in the tertiary sector compared with 10.84 per cent of women across India. The tertiary sector includes jobs in education, health care, transportation, communications, and public administration. Overall, in 1991 about 52 per cent of females in Kerala were employed in the secondary and the tertiary sectors compared with the all-India level of about 19 per cent. The employment patterns of women in Kerala resemble the employment patterns of women in many advanced countries rather than that of India in general.

Census 2001 shows that while fewer women in Kerala are employed as cultivators and agricultural labourers compared with the rest of India, the representation of Kerala women in the category of "other worker" has increased significantly. The census definition of "other workers" includes workers who are employed in government jobs, transportation, banking, social work, teaching, and entertainment. All occupations other than agricultural labourers, cultivators, or household industry workers are included in the "other workers" category. About 67 per cent of the female workforce in Kerala is employed in this sector compared with 21.7 per cent in India. Although detailed classification by nature of jobs would have been helpful to explain this increase, one may speculate that the significantly higher representation of Kerala women in this category may be due to the growth in employment in the tertiary sector.

Main and Marginal Workers by Districts in Kerala

The percentage distribution of total workers by main and marginal category for all the districts in Kerala as shown in Census of India, 2001. The census defines a main worker as someone who has worked for more than six months or 183 days in the preceding year. A marginal worker is a person who has worked for some time but not for the major part of the year. More males are employed as main workers relative to female workers, and generally more female workers in rural areas are employed as main workers relative to urban areas. Across India about 77 per cent of males are employed as main workers, while about 23 per cent of female workers are employed in this category.

An interesting feature among Kerala women is the lower level of participation of women in the marginal worker category compared with men. This is in direct contrast to the general trend among female workers in India, the vast majority of whom opt for casual and marginal labour. According to the 2001 Census, about 60 per cent of women in India are employed as marginal workers compared with 39 per cent of males. When we focus on all the districts in Kerala, we find that fewer females are employed in the marginal category relative to males, and this trend is more pronounced among women in urban districts. Some, however, contend that the demise of many traditional household industries such as handloom and weaving may account for the lower representation of women in the marginal category, at least in the rural areas of Kerala.

The unemployment among females is very high in Kerala compared with the rest of India. This is especially troubling in a state that is characterised by the highest literacy rate and a matrilineal society that confers high status on women. However, when we analyse closely, we find that female workers in Kerala display distinct characteristics that make them outliers compared with the other female workers in India, many of whom are less educated and literate. Fewer women in Kerala are interested in working in the traditionally primary sector as cultivators or agricultural labourers and instead prefer working in the secondary sector and tertiary sector in relatively skilled jobs. While the vast majority of female workers in India are employed as marginal workers, fewer females relative to males in Kerala are employed as marginal workers, despite the high unemployment rate.

Supply Side

Although Kerala has a matrilineal family structure, women's access to education and the nature of their human capital investment are shaped by prevailing social and cultural norms. While Kerala has always been an outlier in India because of its high literacy rate, educational attainment, and human development index, its society has also evolved around male-dominated beliefs and needs that characterise most of India. Thus, the "patrifocal" family structure characterised by the dominance of males in all aspects of life prevails in Kerala despite the existence of the matrilineal mode of family structure.

The educational achievements of women are geared toward their "collective well being", which takes into consideration their roles as wife, mother, and primary caregivers of the family. As a result of this, despite the high literacy rate and educational attainment of women, the nature of human capital investment made by Kerala women is still traditional and geared toward general liberal arts degrees. The prevailing belief is that investment in a general education is beneficial for a woman as it fosters knowledge about education, health, and better child care.

Although such majors translate into occupations that are nontechnical, low paying, and crowded by women, it is not viewed negatively according to the prevailing social norms that still see the man as the primary bread winner and decision maker within the family. Thus, while Kerala is seen as a model state where the gender disparity in literacy rate and education is virtually nonexistent, significant gender disparities exist in the nature of human capital investment. Women in Kerala are still underrepresented in majors that emphasise quantitative, technical, and scientific skills.

Concentration in the sciences and technical fields generally leads to lucrative jobs, yet women in Kerala are discouraged early on from entering such fields because they are not considered suitable in terms of their marriage prospects and future family roles of being a homemaker, wife, mother, and primary caregiver. Social norms thus dictate women's choice of majors in college, their occupational choices, career paths, and subsequently their roles as decision makers at home. The shortage of white-collar jobs has led many women to continue with their schooling and higher education albeit in the same fields in both rural and urban Kerala. About 26 per cent of females were registered as students in rural Kerala; the comparable number for females in rural India was 11 per cent respectively. Thus, growing female enrollment in colleges and universities is partly a reflection of the lower job opportunities for women in the Kerala labour market.

Migration of Males

A large number of male workers have migrated to other countries, primarily to the Gulf countries, in search of meaningful employment. Large-scale emigration to the Gulf countries occurred primarily in the 1970s after the oil boom. As a result, annual remittances received by the wives of the migrant workers have been significant, leaving many families with considerable cash in hand. A large number of women whose household earnings have increased due to remittances from abroad have withdrawn from the labour market. This could be due to individual choices shaped by labour-leisure decisions; alternatively it could also reflect the growing domestic responsibilities of the wife being the sole parent in the household.

In the case of women whose husbands have migrated to other countries, family responsibilities impose significant constraints on their mobility and work responsibilities. At any rate, male migration has affected the reservation wages of many women in the upper and middle classes, many of whom choose to remain unemployed until they find professional jobs to their liking. Women in other parts of India generally do not have such options and often opt for jobs in the secondary labour market.

Job Preferences of Women in Kerala

Neither census nor NSS data give micro-level data based on household or background variables related to the worker. Macro-level data alone are not enough to explain this apparent paradox of high educational attainment and high unemployment among Kerala women. The employment patterns of women in Kerala need to be analysed by incorporating detailed variables about worker and employer characteristics. Few empirical studies have analysed this issue by using micro-level data from Kerala.

In a detailed survey of 502 households, out of which 374 were rural and 128 households were urban, Lakshmy Devi gathered micro-level data related to socio-economic status, education, and employment history of women in Kerala. One important finding was that nearly three-fourths of the unemployed women remained unemployed because of their preferences for skilled white collar jobs. The matrimonial society in Kerala has instilled different aspirations and preferences among the educated women in Kerala, many of whom do not want to be employed marginally or in unskilled work.

Improvements in educational attainment among women have created strong preferences for white-collar and salaried jobs and reduced their willingness to take up manual work or self-employment. Nearly two-thirds of the less educated and more than three-fifths in the educated group wanted to get jobs that were considered socially prestigious. The economic structure, on the other hand, imposes severe constraints on women's employment, as there are not enough skilled jobs.

Demand Side

Structural constraints of the economy, mainly lack of growth of jobs in the manufacturing sector and technical fields, have created an imbalance between demand and supply in the labour market. While there is an abundance of literate and educated females seeking jobs, there are not enough skilled jobs in the labour market. The shortage of white-collar jobs, coupled with discrimination in the labour market, has created a double disadvantage for many women who find it difficult to find suitable employment. The highly educated Kerala women are averse to menial work and prefer jobs that reflect high status in society.

Thus a shortage of white-collar professional jobs coupled with an abundant supply of female graduates with liberal arts degrees partly contributes to the high unemployment rates of females in Kerala. Discrimination in the labour market in a society that still dictates that women have a secondary role in the labour market prevents professional women from experiencing upward mobility in their careers. Perhaps this has a feedback effect on the nature of women's human capital investment.

In the Indian software industry, for example, 60 per cent of women were confined to menial jobs that pay low wages while only 6 per cent were assigned as project managers. According to NSSO data, the proportion of male and female workers changing establishments in order to find different jobs was similar; however, the number of single women workers per 1,000 employed women in urban areas in Kerala changing the status of their jobs was zero. The discriminatory practices of many employers in the private sector may explain the growing trend among women to find employment in the public sector where jobs are more secure and pay non-wage benefits such as pensions. However, jobs in the public sector are scarce and have not kept up with the increasing demand.

In rural Kerala, the opportunities for women to find employment in the agricultural sector has decreased over the past decade and many women are engaged in subsistence work in farms. Many women also work without pay. A micro-level study analysed the role of gender in making important decisions related to farming.

Problems in the Educational System

Although the literacy and educational attainments of women are very high, the quality of education acquired by women in rural areas need to be addressed in order to understand their high unemployment status in the labour market. The quality of higher education needs to improve as many of students cannot compete in national, competitive, and entrance examinations.

At the university level, emphasis is placed more on general education rather than focusing on a curriculum that is in tune with the present needs of the economy. In this global economy, technical skills are very much in demand (IT sector, for example), yet vocational and technical skills are not upgraded in higher education. Typically, the same governments allocates less funding for higher education. The universities and institutions of higher learning also need to be in close contact with the industrial sector in order to maintain a balanced curriculum that keeps pace with modern industrial development and the demand of the marketplace. Colleges and universifies need to revise their course content and curriculum in order to enable educated males and females to find jobs that match their skills in the labour market.

WOMEN EMPOWERMENT THROUGH INFORMATION AND COMMUNICATION TECHNOLOGY

There is hardly any doubt that Information and Communication Technology (ICT), pervades our homes, offices, institutions and our society. Popular, trade, and academic Journals cover developments of ICT weekly and new publications appear to explain or predict the latest trends. But lots of rural areas in India are not yet touched by this ICT.

Though lots of rural people are not yet touched by this ICT, some parts of rural areas are privileged with ICT by the initiatives taken by some NGOs. There is a community of social entrepreneurs and IT companies those are working towards bridging the digital divide.

Rural ICT Programmes

In India special effort was made to provide Community Information Centres (CICs) at block level. Fifty Centres were operational and 487 were planned to be operational. These were located in the most backward region and were geographically difficult.

In Orissa, Mitra Technologies has been working on developing a handicrafts e-trade centre that would connect producers directly to wholesale and retail buyers, resulting in increased efficiencies in marketing and production. This extra-net based computerised network would connect producers to buyers in a B2B environment. Mitra has transformed lives of artisans in Orissa.

Akshaya, the project begun by the Kerala Government has established 565 ICT centres with 5 computers each across Mallapuram district with the aim of familiarising at least one person in every family with computers, besides providing access to e-content in the local language. According to G. R. Kiran, mission coordinator, Kerala State IT Mission, the plan is to set up 9,000 such centres all over Kerala.

The eSwasthya project launched by Bihar Institute of Economic Studies (BIES), on the other hand, would allow the poor in Madhubani district to gain access to better health at lower cost by providing them with smart health cards. These cards would contain their entire health history, which can be accessed at local community health centres.

BIES has signed a contract with IBM Canada Ltd. and Saskatchewan Telecommunications International Inc., in conjunction with BSNL and is being funded by the Canadian International Development Agency (CIDA). A pilot project is being carried out in 22 villages in Madhubani district, said Nitish Mishra, advisor BIES.

Athar Z Haque, Director of the Delhi-based N H Medicomp R & D Pvt Ltd who is managing the e-health-care project in other northern states says that another pilot project is expected to be carried out in 30 villages in Babai tehsil of Hoshangabad district and Khirkiya tehsil of Harda district, both in Madhya Pradesh, who is working in the area of healthcare and is teaching women of her age the use of computers.

NABARD (National Bank of Agriculture and Rural Development) has been operating a programme in Himachal Pradesh with support from the Rural Infrastructure Development Fund (RIDF). This programme has helped to promote both egovernance and e-commerce. There is a similar initiative in Uttarakhand with the help of IIT, Roorkee. Scope for using RIDF in other States should be explored. This will help to convert the concept of every village a knowledge centre into reality.

IT-Mediated Rural Women Education and Dissemination of Health Information: A Pilot Project in Tamil Nadu

The objective of this project is to design and evaluate a web-based education and health information tool targeting rural women in Tamil Nadu, India. This project addresses the United Nations charter for improving the health and social welfare of women in developing countries through education. The project designed, tested and implemented an information technology (IT)-based women education and health information dissemination pilot targeting rural women in the Tiruchirapalli District of Tamil Nadu, India. The project uses existing education infrastructure to demonstrate the economic viability and the social benefits of such a programme in a developing country with complex social and religious interrelationships. A charitable educational institution, the Seethalakshmi Ramaswamy College for Women (SRCW), Tiruchirapalli served as a focal point to educate and disseminate information to rural women.

Target beneficiaries

The beneficiaries of this project are rural women of Tamil Nadu, India, ten rural schools and ten government schools run by the Tiruchirapalli Corporation.

Research results and outcomes

This project was carried out in three phases. The first phase involved a survey in 25 villages and five private schools to assess the level of awareness of health issues such as prenatal care, postnatal care and HIV/AIDS and the importance of school education for students in the target area. Using this information the project developed IT tools for dissemination of information and tested them in the villages and schools. In the second phase the IT tools were modified based on feedback received in phase one. Using the tools, information was disseminated to women and children in about 25 villages that had high school dropout rates and low health awareness, and to young women from two different colleges. The final phase involved coordination with the government for project sustainability.

The pilot has been successful in meeting and surpassing its objectives of raising ICT awareness among young female students in target areas. The project targeted a population in excess of 50,000 in 39 villages and two suburbs of Trichy town. Over 1,000 women from 25 villages participated in various stages of the programme. SRCW trained a group of approximately 200 rural girl students. These results indicate a high, intangible return on investment although the project does note that it is difficult to quantify the impact it has had. The impact can be qualitatively assessed from the response of the participants, which show the project is having a significant impact on raising the awareness of women in these villages. The project notes that those who attend such programmes further spread the message through word of mouth and other informal channels creating a ripple effect that is difficult to quantify.

The project gave the researchers and students insight into where ICTs will work and where they will not. The project notes that women's ability to access health information is impeded by poverty, lack of education, lack of knowledge and resources, social systems, religious beliefs and a variety of other social, economic and political factors. The project sees that the solution to this problem is beyond what a small IT-based project (such as this one) can solve.

IT tools can however play a significant role in distilling information and disseminating it at a reasonable cost, thus providing an effective tool for combating social problems in rural communities. The project felt that a micro-system with local community ownership could be a forerunner to similar ones in other parts of India. Subsequent to this project, the researchers proposed to communicate these findings to State Government authorities and to discuss strategies for further implementation. The researchers note that one year was probably too short a time to make a substantial impact.

4

Rural Women and Health

In India, 120 million women live in poverty. India has 16 per cent of the world's population, but only 2.4 per cent of its land, resulting in great pressures on its natural resources. Over 70 per cent of India's population currently derive their livelihood from land resources, which includes 84 per cent of the economically-active women.

India is one of the few countries where males significantly outnumber females, and this imbalance has increased over time. India's maternal mortality rates in rural areas are among the world's highest. From a global perspective, Indian accounts for 19 per cent of all lives births and 27 per cent of all maternal deaths.

There seems to be a consensus that higher female mortality between ages one and five and high maternal mortality rates result in a deficit of females in the population. Studies estimates that deaths of young girls in India exceed those of young boys by over 300,000 each year, and every sixth infant death is specifically due to gender discrimination." Of the 15 million baby girls born in India each year, nearly 25 per cent will not live to see their 15th birthday.

India's total fertility rate of 3.8 births per woman can be considered moderate by world standards, but the sheer magnitude of population increase has resulted in such a feeling of urgency that containment of population growth is listed as one of the six most important objectives in the Eighth Five-Year Plan.

Since 1970, the use of modern contraceptive methods has risen from 10 per cent to 40 per cent, with great variance between northern and southern India. The most striking aspect of contraceptive use in India is the predominance of sterilisation, which accounts for more than 85 per cent of total modern contraception use, with female sterilisation accounting for 90 per cent of all sterilisations.

The Indian constitution grants women equal rights with men, but strong patriarchal traditions persist, with women's lives shaped by customs that are centuries old. In most Indian families, a daughter is viewed as a liability, and she is conditioned to believe that she is inferior and subordinate to men. Sons are idolised and celebrated. *May you be the mother of a hundred sons* is a common Hindu wedding blessing.

A study of women in the Swayam Shikshan Prayog (SSP), based in 20 villages in four districts in Maharashtra state was introduced in this way:

The primary issue all women in the SSP were struggling with was that of everyday survival. Insufficient incomes and the lack of employment were reported to be their most pressing concerns. Survival is a constant preoccupation and at its most basic, survival means food. The most common problems were the lack of basic amenities such as food, water, fuel, fodder and health facilities. In addition, the deterioration of the natural environment and the fact that many of their traditional occupations were no longer viable were conditions that were making it increasingly hard for women to continue sustaining their families, as they had done in the past.

SSP is a loose, informal network of women's collectives, voluntary organisations, action groups and unions.

WOMEN ARE MALNOURISHED

The exceptionally high rates of malnutrition in South Asia are rooted deeply in the soil of inequality between men and women. Gender disparities in nutrition are evident from infancy to adulthood. In fact, gender has been the most statistically significant determinant of malnutrition among young children and malnutrition is a frequent direct or underlying cause of death among girls below age 5. Girls are breast-fed less frequently and for shorter durations in infancy; in childhood and adulthood, males are fed first and better. Adult women consume approximately 1,000 fewer calories per day than men according to one estimate from Punjab. Comparison of household dietary intake studies in different parts of the country shows that nutritional equity between males and females is lower in northern than in southern states.

Nutritional deprivation has two major consequences for women: they never reach their full growth potential and anaemia. Both are risk factors in pregnancy, with anaemia ranging from 40-50 per cent in urban areas to 50-70 per cent in rural areas. This condition complicates childbearing and result in maternal and infant deaths, and low birth weight infants.

One study found anaemia in over 95 per cent of girls ages 6-14 in Calcutta, around 67 per cent in the Hyderabad area, 73 per cent in the New Delhi area, and about 18 per cent in the Madras area. This study states, "The prevalence of anaemia among women ages 15-24 and 25-44 years follows similar patterns and levels. Besides posing risks during pregnancy, anaemia increases women's susceptibility to diseases such as tuberculosis and reduces the energy women have available for daily activities such as household chores, child care, and agricultural labour. Any severely anaemic individual is taxed by most physical activities, including walking at an ordinary pace.

WOMEN ARE IN POOR HEALTH

Surviving through a normal life-cycle is a resource-poor woman's greatest challenge. The practice of breast-feeding female children for shorter periods of time reflects the strong desire for sons. If women are particularly anxious to have a male child, they may deliberately try to become pregnant again as soon as possible after a female is born. Conversely, women may consciously seek to avoid another pregnancy after the birth of a male child in order to give maximum attention to the new son.

A primary way that parents discriminate against their girl children is through neglect during illness. When sick, little girls are not taken to the doctor as frequently as are their brothers. A study in Punjab shows that medical expenditures for boys are 2.3 times higher than for girls.

As adults, women get less health care than men. They tend to be less likely to admit that they are sick and they'll wait until their sickness has progressed before they seek help or help is sought for them. Studies on attendance at rural primary health centers reveal that more males than females are treated in almost all parts of the country, with differences greater in northern hospitals than southern ones, pointing to regional differences in the value placed on women. Women's socialisation to tolerate suffering and their reluctance to be examined by male personnel are additional constraints in their getting adequate health care.

MATERNAL MORTALITY

India's maternal mortality rates in rural areas are among the highest in the world. A factor that contributes to India's high maternal mortality rate is the reluctance to seek medical care for pregnancy — it is viewed as a temporary condition that will disappear. The estimates nationwide are that only 40-50 per cent of women receive any antenatal care. Evidence from the states of Bihar, Rajasthan, Orissa, Uttar Pradesh, Maharashtra and Gujarat find registration for maternal and child health services to be as low as 5-22 per cent in rural areas and 21-51 per cent in urban areas.

Even a woman who has had difficulties with previous pregnancies is usually treated with home remedies only for three reasons: the decision that a pregnant woman seek help rests with the mother-in-law and husband; financial considerations; and fear that the treatment may be more harmful than the malady.

It is estimated that pregnancy-related deaths account for one-quarter of all fatalities among women aged 15 to 29, with well over two-thirds of them considered preventable. For every maternal death in India, an estimated 20 more women suffer from impaired health. One village-level study of rural women in Maharashtra determined on the basis of physical examinations that some 92 per cent suffered from one or more gynecological disorder.

Contraception Use

Women's health is harmed by lack of access to and the poor quality of reproductive services. About 24.6 million couples, representing roughly 18 per cent of all married women, want no more children but are not using contraception. The causes of this unmet need remain poorly understood, but a qualitative study in Tamil Nadu suggests that women's lack of decision-making power in the family, opportunity costs involved in seeking contraception, fear of child death, and poor quality of contraceptive service all play an important role.

Impact of Job on Maternal Health

The tasks performed by women are usually those that require them to be in one position for long periods of time, which can adversely affect their reproductive health. A study in a rice-growing belt of coastal Maharashtra found that 40 per cent of all infant deaths occurred in the months of July to October. The study also found that a majority of births were either premature or stillbirths. The study attributed this to the squatting position that had to be assumed during July and August, the rice transplanting months.

The impact of pollution and industrial wastes on health is considerable. The smoke from household biomass (made up of wood, dung and crop residues) stoves within a three-hour period is equivalent to smoking 20 packs of cigarettes. For women who spend at least three hours per day cooking, often in a poorly ventilated area, the impact includes eye problems, respiratory problems, chronic bronchitis and lung cancer. One study quoted by WHO found that pregnant women cooking over open biomass stoves had almost a 50 per cent higher chance of stillbirth.

Anaemia makes a person more susceptible to carbon monoxide toxicity, which is one of the main pollutants in the biomass smoke. Given the number of Indian women who are anaemic — 25 to 30 per cent in the reproductive age group and almost 50 per cent in the third trimester — this adds to their vulnerability to carbon monoxide toxicity.

Additionally, with an increasing population, diseases caused by waste disposal, such as hookworm, are rampant. People who work barefooted are particularly susceptible, and it has been found that hookworm is directly responsible for the high percentage of anaemia among rural women.

Maternal Health Policies

Maternal health is almost always seen as a technical and health issue which means that the medical establishment is regarded as best qualified to speak on it. Policy making on maternal health has therefore never consulted those who are directly affected, that is the women who undergo pregnancy. Policies and Five Year Plans set ambitious targets to reduce maternal mortality, but programmes continue to look away from women. Women have never been consulted on where they prefer to give birth, what support they need for their choices, what happens when they seek help, and what their experience have been in seeking abortions. Neither have women been asked whether all their pregnancies are of choice, whether they need more support in making reproductive decisions and whether they can actually exercise sexual choices and sexual health protection.

Today, policy making is also largely dictated by concerns of cost, since health care is rapidly becoming a lucrative industry rather than a right. In the name of being 'cost effective', however, often highly technical, unrealistic and cost-intensive solutions may be promoted. One classic example is the promotion of compulsory 'institutional delivery' for every birth as the only solution for averting maternal deaths. Despite the fact that women may see birth as a private activity to be carried out in the comfort of home or that there are birth attendants in most communities who can be given more training, policy makers insist that all women should deliver in hospitals. This is despite the knowledge that only 15% of all births lead to complications and the rest are normal deliveries and that complications can happen in the ninth month of pregnancy or up to six weeks after delivery. Policy makers set aside the evident fact that large numbers of women cannot afford the travel costs and informal payments for undergoing birth in state-run institutions: more importantly, that in large parts of India there are no institutions or referral systems to handle the complicated cases! Knowing all this, policy makers have preferred to promote institutional delivery through incentive payments and other means.

A group of Indian NGOs working with directly affected women decided that they would take women to directly voice their concerns and their experiences regarding their right to maternal health to address the policy makers in the country's capital. A three-day policy dialogue took place in New Delhi on 27-29 December 2005, called "VOICES FROM THE GROUND: Policy Dialogues on Women's Right to Maternal Health," organised by SAHAYOG (Lucknow), CHETNA (Ahmedabad) and the Centre for Health and Social Justice (New Delhi), which was attended by 100 participants from eight states of India (apart from local media persons). These dialogues enabled rural and urban low-income women to directly address the media, Ministry and Planning Commission officials and donors regarding their demands for the improvement of maternal health services in India.

The rural women presented testimonies of their experience of seeking maternal health care, denial of health services and described maternal deaths in their families Supporting the women were a number of NGOs who had jointly drafted a set of concrete recommendations for the government. The NGOs supporting the women gave evidence from various parts of the country to indicate that maternal health services were highly inequitable, with a 'clustering of deaths' in certain states, among poor rural women and among Dalit and tribal women.

The Ministry of Health and Family Welfare (Government of India) responded to the women by asking for detailed descriptions of the maternal death cases so that some action could be taken, and this was followed up by a series of faxes from the participating NGOs to the Ministry. Fortunately, the officials have taken action and enquiry letters were issued in 2006. The Ministry also invited the organisers to present these testimonies at three state-level meetings on maternal health (in states with high maternal mortality), so as to bring home the immediacy of the problem to officials at the state level.

However, the rural women and NGOs from Uttar Pradesh wanted to create more pressure from the 'demand side', as they had been documenting denial of maternal health services, doing case work and carrying on the dialogue with state officials for two years already. They felt there was need for a more concerted state-level campaign to raise awareness within the community and the government regarding women's right to maternal health. Rural women decided to call the campaign Complete Citizens Total Rights Campaign (Poori Nagrik, Poora Haq) and this was carried out over several districts of Uttar Pradesh from 6th March to 28th May 2006.

The rural women and NGOs collected around 35,000 signatures supporting their demands and took them to the Minister of Family Welfare on the eve of 28 May 2006 (International Day of Action for Women's Health). They met the local health officials in their districts and presented their problems, indicating their demands for maternal health rights through a poster. Women also monitored the implementation of the government's Rural Health Mission and gave feedback to the state's Director General of Family Welfare at a meeting to celebrate the first anniversary of the Mission launch.

The rural women also met members of the State Commission for Women and made presentations inside the State Legislative Assembly. They marched in colourful processions, carrying a 'woman's corpse' to symbolise maternal death, and they stood dressed in shrouds with candles to protest against the forty thousand maternal deaths in the Uttar Pradesh state each year.

The outcome was that the Minister of Family Welfare began to make announcements in the media regarding the importance of maternal health. In some districts, the local health officials developed improved relations with NGOs and enlisted their support in implementing the National Rural Health Mission. The rural women themselves declared the launch of a state-level organisation to continue working on the issue of women's right to maternal health.

These two efforts indicate that women are able to clearly articulate their needs and preferences on maternal health services despite being non-literate, rural and from low-income families. Women are directly affected by health policies, and their experiences and their choices should form the content of policy deliberations, rather than only the technical medical point of view, which often overlooks the social and economic context within which maternity occurs. As we move towards a rights-based approach in maternal health, women's voices need to be given more space, and women's choices need to be considered in decision-making.

Maternal Health Programme

Promotion of maternal and child health has been one of the most important objectives of the Family Welfare Programme in India. The current Reproductive and Child Health Programme (RCH) was launched in October 1997. The RCH Programme incorporates the components covered under the Child Survival and Safe Motherhood Programme and includes an additional component relating to reproductive tract infection and sexually transmitted infections. In order to improve maternal health at the community level a cadre of community level skilled birth attendant who will attend to the pregnant women in the community is being considered.

The need for bringing down maternal mortality rate significantly and improving maternal health in general has been strongly stressed in the National Population Policy 2000. This policy recommends a holistic strategy for bringing about total intersectoral coordination at the grass root level and involving the NGOs, Civil Societies, Panchayati Raj Institutions and Women's Group in bringing down Maternal Mortality Ratio and Infant Mortality Rate.

Maternal Mortality Ratio

Over a 100,000 women in India continue to die of pregnancy related causes every year. The Maternal Mortality Ratio in India is 407 per 100,000 live births. The major causes of these deaths have been identified as hemorrhage (both ante and post partum), toxemia (Hypertension during pregnancy), anemia, obstructed labour, puerperal sepsis (infections after delivery) and unsafe abortion.

Maternal Mortality is a cause of great concern. However, reliable estimates of maternal mortality are not available. Any intervention to check it will only be effective if we know reasonably accurate data on maternal mortality. An expert group has been constituted in the Department of Family Welfare, which is looking into the modalities of carrying out a survey for collection of data on Maternal Mortality. A Pilot Survey for this has already been completed.

Interventions

Reduction of maternal mortality is an important goal. The Department of Family Welfare has took several new initiatives, during the current Plan period, to make the programme broad based and client friendly. The focus was, accordingly, shifted from individualised vertical interventions to a more holistic and integrated life-cycle approach giving more focused attention to the reproductive health care. The Maternal Health Programme which is a component of the Reproductive and Child Health Programme aims at reducing maternal mortality to less than 100 by the 2010. The major interventions includes:

Essential obstetric care

Essential obstetric care intends to provide the basic maternity services to all pregnant women. The RCH Programme aims at providing at least 3 antenatal check ups during which weight and blood pressure check, abdominal examination, immunisation against tetanus, iron and folic acid prophylaxis as well as anemia management are provided to the pregnant women. In Uttar Pradesh and Bihar, the content and quality of antenatal care was poor as compared to Haryana and Tamil Nadu.

Emergency obstetric care

Complications associated with pregnancies are not

always predictable. Therefore, emergency obstetric care is an important intervention to prevent maternal morbidity and mortality. Under the RCH Programme, efforts are being made to strengthen the emergency Obstetric Care Services and make the FRUs operational.

Under the RCH Programme FRUs are also being strengthened through supply of drugs in the form of emergency obstetric drug kits and skilled manpower on contractual and hiring basis. The sub-district hospitals, CHCs and FRUs are entitled to hire services of Private Anesthetists for conducting emergency operations for which they are to be paid Rs.1000 per case. Rs.83.73 lakhs have been released to the States; however, Private Anaesthetists have been hired only for 1059 operations so far.

24-Hours Delivery Services at PHCs/CHCs

To promote institutional deliveries, provision has been made under the current RCH Programme to give additional honorarium to the staff to encourage round the clock delivery services at PHCs and CHCs. This is to ensure that at least one medical officer, nurse, and cleaner is available beyond normal working hours. Under this scheme Rs.1168.88 lakhs have been released to 21 States based on the proposals received from them.

Referral Transport

Time is an important factor for obstetric emergencies. Women who undergo deliveries at home and develop complications often find it difficult to be transported to a referral unit. Under the current RCH Programme Provision has been made to assist women from indigent families in 25% of the sub-centre in selected States to provide a lump sum corpus fund to Panchayat through District Family Welfare Officers. Since 2000-2001, the scheme has been extended to all the States and UTs. Rs.595.65 lakhs have been released 16 States based on the proposals received from them.

Safe Abortion Services

Abortion is a significant medical and social problem worldwide. It is estimated that half the abortions taking place around the world every year are performed outside authorised health services and or by unauthorised often unskilled providers and most take place in the developing world. Whether spontaneous or induced, abortion has been a matter of concern over many decades now, particularly because of sepsis and other complications which lead to maternal morbidity and mortality. In India, abortion is a major cause of maternal death and accounts for 8.9% of maternal mortality every year.

The Medical Termination of Pregnancy Act, 1971

The Medical Termination of Pregnancy Act, 1971 has been under implementation since 1972. Over the years, the number of centre where pregnancy can be terminated has increased and at present there are 11025 recognised MTP clinics in the country. However, considering the fact that a large number of unsafe abortions still take place providing for more facilitie for MTP services has been taken into consideration under the ongoing Reproductive and Child Health Programme.

Efforts are being made to provide for the unmet need of safe abortion services and to improve utilisation of existing facilities and further expand the MTP facilities so as to make safe abortion services accessible to all women in the country including the women in rural areas. At present, Government of India under the RCH programme is undertaking training of medical personnel in MTP technique, and undertaking IEC activities for improving the awareness and knowledge of the community. The MTP Act, 1971 has also been amended with the objective of delegating power to a Committee at the district level to facilitate recognition of more centres where MTPs can be undertaken.

Amendments to the Act

The provision of the Act has now been amended to delegate the powers for approval of places, from the States to the District level through a committee headed by Chief Medical Officer or District Health Officer.

Amendment to MTP Rules

1. Medical Method of Abortion – Termination of early pregnancy with two drugs Mifepristone (RU 486) and Misoprostol have undergone extensive research and is considered extremely safe under supervision with appropriate counseling. Use of Mifepristone followed by Misoprostol is an established and safe method for terminating early pregnancy. In April 2002, Drug Controller of India approved marketing of Mifepristone for termination of early pregnancy, a method also known as Medical Abortion. Currently its use in India is recommended upto 7 weeks (49 days of amenorrhea) in a facility with provision for safe abortion services and blood transfusion.
2. Termination of early pregnancy with RU 486 and Misoprostol is offered to women under the purview of the MTP Act, 1971 and Rules 2003 which specify to whom, by whom and where pregnancy is to be terminated.
3. Manual Vacuum Aspiration (MVA): The Department of Family Welfare is considering the

introduction of Manual Vacuum Aspiration (MVA) technique in the Family Welfare Programme. Manual Vacuum Aspiration is a safe and simple technique for termination of early pregnancy that makes it feasible to be used in Primary Health Centres or comparable facilities, thereby increasing access to safe abortion services. The project of introducing the MVA technique is being piloted in two identified districts of each of the eight selected states initially.

4. The pilot project is being coordinated by FOGSI and implemented in collaboration with the Ministry of Health and FW, respective State Governments, WHO and FOGSI. In each district 8-10 doctors alongwith their accompanying staff nurses or Lady Health Visitors will be trained.
5. Prevention and Management of Reproductive Tract Infection (RTI) and Sexually Transmitted Infections (STI).
6. Reproductive Tract Infections pose grave threats to women's Life throughout the world. RTI includes sexually transmitted infection, men also experience RTIs but prevalence and a consequence for women are much more severe. Services for the prevention and treatment of RTI/STI are integral part of the Reproductive Child Health Programme. All community based prevalence studies of women and men's health conducted in India indicate that rates of RTI are very high.
7. RTI/STI linked to HIV/AIDS, therefore, the planning and implementation of services for RTI/STI has been done in close collaboration with National AIDS Control Organisation (NACO). All STD clinics at the district level are being assisted by NACO while incorporating the RTI component.

The assistance from Govt. of India is in the form of training, laboratory equipments, RTI/STI drug kit and financial assistance for disposable laboratory items.

8. *Integrated Financial Envelop*: Under the RCH Programme flexibility was granted to the four southern States of Tamil Nadu, Andhra Pradesh, Karnataka, Maharashtra and Kerala and Punjab. The purpose of the envelope is to provide flexibility to better performing States to design package of interventions to address problems of Maternal Health Care instead of tying them to national schemes. An amount of Rs.2085.92 lakhs have been released to these six States.
9. *Training of Dais*: 10. A scheme for training of Dais was initiated during 2001-02. The scheme is being implemented in 156 districts in 18 States/UTs of the country. The districts have been selected on the basis of the safe delivery rates being less than 30%. The Scheme has been extended to all the districts of EAG States i.e. Bihar, Orissa, Madhya Pradesh, Rajasthan, Uttarakhand, Uttar Pradesh, Jharkhand and Chhatisgarh. On the request of the State Governments the scheme has also been extended to Andaman & Nicobar Island and more districts of J&K. The aim is to train at least one Dai in every village with the objective of making deliveries safe. Till date, Rs.881.30 lakhs have been released to the States and 59,296 Dais have been trained so far under this Scheme.
11. The endeavour of the Department of Family Welfare is also to implement Dai Training projects through NGOs. Funds amounting to Rs.27.56 lakhs were released for Dai Training to two mother NGOs during March, 2000. They have completed

training of 1990 Dais in their project area. During 2001-02, an amount of Rs.49.22 lakhs have been released to eight NGOs for undertaking training of Dais.

12. *RCH Camps*: In order to provide the RCH services to people living in remote areas where the existing services are underutilised, a scheme for holding camps have been initiated during the year 2001. The scheme is implemented in the 10 weak states and also in the Eastern States. Report received from the States suggested that the scheme is well appreciated in the Rural Community and large number of people is attending these camps. On the request of the State Governments, the scheme has been extended to 76 additional districts during 2001-02 for which an amount of Rs.1887.40 lakhs to the States have been released. According to the information received from different States, 7283 camps have been organised in the States upto date.

As a result of these interventions, a recent survey results of which have come for 50% of the districts indicates that Institutional Delivery has increased from 33.6% (NFHS-II) to 46.9% and Safe Delivery has increased from 42.3% (NFHS-II) to 62.1%.

New initiatives

Training of MBBS doctors in Anesthetic Skills for Emergency Obstetric Care at FRUs.

To alleviate shortage of specialist manpower Government of India launched. Training of MBBS doctors for gaining Anaesthetic Skills in Emergency Obstetric Care at FRUs. The 18 weeks training Programme for the first batch has been pilot tested at AIIMS and will soon be disseminated to the States.

Obstetric Management Skills

Government of India is also considering introducing training of MBBS doctors in Obstetric Management Skills. Federation of Obstetric and Gynecological Society of India has prepared the training for 16 weeks in all obstetric management skills including Caesarian Section operation and is at present under consideration.

Setting up of Blood Storage Centers (BSC) at FRUs

Timely treatment for complications associated with pregnancy is sometimes hampered due to non-availability of Blood Transfusion services at FRUs to facilitate establishment of Blood Storage Centers at such FRUs the Drugs and Cosmetics Act have been amended and guidelines for these Blood Storage Centers (BSCs), have been prepared and disseminated to the States. Initial funding and equipment will be provided by Government of India under RCH-II.

Developing a cadre of Community Level Skilled Birth Attendant

The major causes of maternal deaths are due to hemorrhage (ante partum and post partum), anemia, infection, unsafe abortion, obstructed labour and hypertensive disorders of pregnancy. A large number of these causes are preventable through improved maternal care and ensuring appropriate treatment of complications, ideally all the deliveries should be conducted by trained health functionaries, however, presently the health care system is not in a position to provide all pregnant women, services of a trained health functionary at the time of delivery. Therefore there is a need for developing a cadre of Community level skilled birth attendant who will attend to the pregnant women in the community.

A 'Community Level Skilled Birth Attendant' is a

person who will be trained in midwifery to provide maternal care at the community level. She will be selected from the community where she will set up her practice after completion of her training of one year in midwifery. The community level skilled birth attendant will not be a financial or administrative obligation to the health system in any way. They will be left in the villages to practice the skills provided. They will serve in the same community for a minimum period of three years and will not be given government services. They will be given stipend for the training period and hostel facility will be provided at ANM training centres. This scheme will be taken up during Phase II of RCH Programme.

Janani Suraksha Yojana

The scheme is a modification of National Maternity Benefit Scheme, referral transport etc. and is at present under consideration.

Objectives

— Reduction in MMR & IMR
— Focus on Institutional Delivery

Features

— Encouraging Small Family Norms
— Provision for Caesarean Section
— Encouraging Pregnant Women to Undergo Tubectomy/Laparoscopy
— Trained TBA to be Effective Link Between Field Level Health Functionary & the BPL Woman
— Payment Of Incentive to Dai/ASHA
— Fund to be Released Through State SCOVAS/State Department of Family Welfare

— Benefit to be Disbursed by ANM through Recoupable imprest

Graded Benefits

— Assistance to mother increased to Rs. 700 in rural areas of Low Performing States (>25%) and Rs. 600 to Urban areas of LPS & Rural areas of HPS (<25%).

— Assistance package of Rs. 600 in Rural Area for Institutional Delivery in low Performing States to meet Dai/ASHA fee, transport cost and food and incidental charges during delivery.

— In Urban Areas of LPS, the assistance package is limited to Rs. 200.

Accredited Social Health Activist (ASHA)

Government of India has recently announced a National Rural Health Mission (NRHM) with a clear goal of addressing the health needs of rural population especially vulnerable sections of the society. Such community level link workers may be called as Accredited Social Health Activists (ASHAs). ASHA will act as a link among beneficiary at village level, Anganwadi Worker and ANM. The scheme is under consideration.

Initially it is planned to give this helper (ASHA) to all the villages of EAG States, Assam and J & K. She will help and guide women to assess the health facilities for Anti-natal care, Institutional delivery, post-natal care and counseling on nutrition and Family Planning Services.

Vande Matram Scheme

The scheme is continuing under Public Private Partnership with the involvement of Federation of Obstetric and Gynaecological Society of India and Private

Clinics. The aim of the scheme is to reduce the maternal mortality and morbidity of the pregnant and expectant mothers by involving and utilising the vast resources of specialists/trained work force available in the private sector. The scheme intends to provide free antenatal and postnatal check, counseling on nutrition, breastfeeding, spacing of birth etc. through public private partnership.

This is a voluntary scheme wherein any OBG specialist, maternity home, nursing home can volunteer themselves in joining the scheme. Any lady doctor/ MBBS doctor providing safe motherhood services can also volunteer to join this scheme. The enrolled 'Vandematram' doctors will display 'Vandematram' logo in their clinic, Iron and Folic Acid Tablets, oral pills, TT injections etc. will be provided by the respective District Medical Officers to the 'Vandematram' doctors/clinics for free distributions to beneficiaries. The cases needing special care and treatment can be referred to the Government Hospitals and institutes, who have been advised to take due care to the patients coming with Vandematram cards. The details of the scheme, reporting format etc. are available with District Medical Officers and Director of Family Welfare in the States.

Operationalisation of Primary Health Facilities under Reproductive and Child Health Programme (RCH-2nd Phase)

RCH Programme which started in the year 1997-98 is likely to end by the March 2005. From 1st April, 2005 RCH 2nd phase is likely to begin and at this stage the programme is under consideration for approval. The focus of the programme will be to reduce the Maternal & Child Mortality & Morbidity with emphasis on rural health care. This time more flexibility have been given to the States for planning their own interventions for achieving the goals, accordingly the states have been requested to make their own project implementation plan with indications for achieving the desired milestones.

Under RCH Phase-II, it is envisaged to operationalise about 2000 FRUs for providing Emergency Obstetric Care. Besides this all CHCs & 50% of the PHCs are to be made functional for providing 24 Hrs. delivery services.

WOMEN'S HEALTH PROBLEMS: A BRIEF STUDY IN KERALA

Kerala had high development indicators not just confined to economic wealth. The state had been witnessing a demographic transition with the elderly constituting almost more than 50% of the population. Birth rates and death rates had lowered and life expectancy has increased. The literacy rates of women were high. Fertility rate had declined and the state could boast of successful use of family planning methods. Due to the efficacy of people's plan campaign, people had succeeded in getting electricity and toilet facilities.

However, these development indicators masked many of the underlying realities of the state with respect to the status and situation of women. For example, as far as school attendance was concerned, the rates were the similar for boys and girls. These however started decreasing at the higher secondary level with girls starting to work as domestic helpers and boys stopping studies to earn income. As far as work participation rates were concerned, Kerala occupied the 19th position with women's work participation rate as low as 15.3%. Though very early marriages below 15 years were not common, regional differences existed.

According to NFHS data, universal marriages of women existed in Kerala. Majority of the women who were divorced, deserted and separated were those who were above the age of 60 years. 46% of women above 80 years were widowed or had lost their husbands, while only 7% of men about 80 years had lost their wives. The elderly population in Kerala, especially women who had been widowed, divorced and separated had a number of economic, social as well as health problems, which continued to be unaddressed at the policy level. The mean age of marriage of women was 21 years. There was an average 6 years of difference between the age at marriage between man and women in the state. It was also seen that 78% houses are male-headed, whereas only 22% houses continued to be female headed.

Data on women's utilisation of health care services showed that the utilisation was very high for care related to pregnancy and childbirth such as ante-natal care during pregnancy, where the percentage of women seeking health care was as high as 94 to 99%. Almost 100% of the deliveries in Kerala were institutional with 88% of the deliveries taking place in private hospitals. A few cases of home deliveries were found in Malappuram and Palakkad districts, which were socio-economically backward as compared to other districts.

However, these indicators based on rates and ratios masked the realities in the state and provide an incomplete picture of the health situation of women in the state. For example, inspite of the uniform distribution of health services; there were instances of maternal mortality in the state. However, no records existed for these maternal mortalities. There was a need to conduct an audit of maternal mortality deaths in the state. IMR rates in Kerala were comparable with those of Sweden and Britain, but MMR rates were comparable with Bihar and other northern states.

There were regional differences in immunisation with 48% in Malappuram and 100% in Kollam and Ernakulam. 61% of the people were dependent on the public sector for immunisation.

Use of MTP as a method of abortion seemed to be reducing with more and more women opting for medical abortion as a convenient means to abort the foetus. According to the study conducted by Achutha Menon Centre, women depended on the private sector for first trimester abortions and on the public sector for second trimester abortions.

The recent NFHS data showed that 29% of women had caesarean deliveries. Many of these were conducted in private clinics. Why did it happen more in private institutions was a question that needed consideration while looking at the health issues of women in the state.

In addition to the above problems, women from Kerala had also been found to be suffering from a number of noncommunicable diseases. For example, the incidence of Breast Cancer and Thyroid Cancer was high in the state. Women in Kerala also suffered from obesity and 55% had hypertension due to changes in life style. Diabetes was also on the increase among women. Chronic obstructive lung diseases were on the increase due to 80% dependence on wood as cooking fuel. Smoking rate was below 2%, but tobacco chewing in women was high in Kerala. However, no systematic studies existed that looked at the impact of tobacco consumption on the health of women.

Mental illness among women in the state had been found to be much higher than the national average. Suicide rates among married women were higher in Kerala in contrast to that of women in developed countries, where suicide rates were higher among unmarried women. However, numbers of actual deaths in men were higher compared to reported attempted suicide rates in women. Family suicides were also on the rise in the state due to indebtedness and increase in wants due to changes in life styles.

Violence against women was high within homes and harassment in public spheres was higher than that of other states. In a study conducted by Sakhi, 36% women had faced some kind of violence. 11% in between the age of 15 to 17 years had faced sexual abuse at some point of time.

Due to reproductive span of 8 to 9 years and less reliance on contraceptive methods and emphasis on sterilisation among women, women were at a very high risk of suffering from HIV/AIDS. However, messages in the HIV/AIDS programmes continued to ignore the gender-related issues leading to increased vulnerability of women to HIV/AIDS. The messages continued to propagate stereotypical images of the roles of women such as be faithful to your husband, abstinence and use of condoms without taking into consideration the sociocultural contexts of the women. For example, the use of condoms continued to be impracticable in the state and among women because of lack of say and sexual negotiation capacities among women besides other practical considerations such as disposal of the condoms.

A number of reproductive health problems not related to pregnancy and childbirth also continued to be common among women and needed attention. For example, morbidities reported after sterilisations among women continued to be high and were found to be related to the poor quality of services in the state. Other gynaecological morbidities such as menstrual problems, reproductive tract infections, sexually transmitted infections, urinary tract infections continued to be high among women in the state and needed attention. Other problems such as prolapse of the uterus, infertility though frequently reported by women, continued to be poorly researched in the state. In spite of the high rate of hysterectomies among women in the state, no studies existed on hysterectomies among women.

Infertility among women was also a problem in Kerala. There was pressure on the women to conceive within one year of marriage. Though sperm count was coming down among men, men were not prepared to talk about their infertility problem. The proportion of secondary infertility caused by reproductive tract infection and tubal infection was also high in the state.

Maternal Mortality

Maternal Mortality Ratio is referred to as number of maternal deaths per 100,000 livebirths. Ratio is appropriate as it includes the number of deaths regardless of pregnancy outcome (livebirths, stillbirths and ectopic pregnancies, abortions) while the denominator includes only live births.

According to the recent estimates by WHO a mother dies from complications in pregnancy and childbirth every minute. In a day 1400 mothers die, while in one year more than 50,000 mothers die. Globally, for every two people who die in traffic accidents, one mother and 20 children die from preventable and treatable causes.

Of the deaths, 99% of maternal deaths occur in low and middle-income countries, particularly in sub-Saharan Africa and South Asia. Within each country, mothers and children from the poorest families are the most likely to die.

India with a population of 1.03 Billion and annual growth rate of 1.6% and Gross National Per Capita Inc.<745 USD contributes in terms of 136,000 maternal deaths (largest number of maternal deaths).

According to the Millennium Development goals, the 5th goal is to improve maternal health. The reasons for deaths due to maternal mortality have been highlighted in the High Risk Concept includes the understanding that Too Many, too close, too young, too old and too late, who suffer from infectious diseases such as malaria, TB and HIV/AIDS, and who are malnourished or anaemic die but now we know that, More women in low risk die simply because more deliver in low risk group. Hence Every pregnancy is at risk

Women from low income countries are more at risk because of the following factors High fertility, anaemia, immune deficiency, malnutrition, poor transport facilities, lack of blood transfusion facility, deliveries by untrained personnel, illegal abortions. However, in many of the cases, these deaths can be preventable. For example, looking at the location of women at the time of deaths, it can be seen that 41% women die within homes, 50% in hospitals, while 9% die in transit.

Women die during transit even in a state such as Kerala, which has the lowest MMR in the country. Delays in problem recognition and decision-making, delays in reaching the referral facilities and delays in getting care at the health facility have been identified as three important reasons leading to maternal deaths in developing countries.

The direct causes (directly due to complications of pregnancy, labour & peurperium) of maternal deaths constitute 80% of the deaths and include deaths due to Pre eclampsia/eclampsia, hemorrhage, sepsis, rupture of the uterus, embolism, unsafe abortions. Indirect causes constitute 20% of the deaths and include conditions such as heart disease, hepatic disease, anaemia, malaria, acute infected conditions, GI diseases and malnutrition.

Haemorrhage is the highest cause worldwide followed by sepsis, unsafe abortions and eclampsia. In Kerala, haemorrhage continues to be most important cause for maternal mortality in 2000, with the major cause of death being sepsis in the 90s, sepsis and criminal abortions in the 80's, and haemorrhage in the 1960s as well.

Even though Kerala has low MMR, every maternal death is preventable and should be prevented. The following steps can be taken to reduce the maternal deaths: Every pregnancy should be registered to reduce complications and avert maternal deaths. Educating women and improving awareness regarding health, improving emergency obstretic care, improving quality of antenatal care, improving maternal audits can go a long way in preventing maternal deaths.

The recommendations to prevent MMR include:

— Prevention of pregnancy by adopting FP measures like female sterilisation and small family norm,

— Legalisation of abortion and improving the access to safe abortion services from both government and private facilities,

— Increase awareness among women

— Make medical abortion easily available.

Health of Tribals in Kerala

The tribals who formed one of the marginalised communities in the state and suffered from a number of illnesses such as sickle cell anaemia, thyroid disorder, cancers, addiction related disorders. Contagious diseases such as cholera, viral fever, jaundice and TB were also common among tribals. Social changes had also affected the traditional practices of the tribals. Thus, immigration, population pressures, lack of facilities to maintain proper hygiene, lack of educational facilities and awareness, changes in cultivation patterns and environmental degradation had affected the ooru system of the tribals.

Marginalisation, poor infrastructural facilities, neglect at the policy level, isolation, poor acceptance of family planning and contraception, illiteracy, traditional beliefs systems and practices led to a number of health problems among men and women. Addiction was a common problem among both men and women. The need to direct attention at the plight of the tribals, increasing awareness and rapport among the tribal populations by communicating with them in their own language, understanding their culture and traditions, providing infrastructural facilities, improving health services and attention at the policy level were highlighted as important steps to improve the situation of the tribals.

Illiteracy was high among the tribals with it being 41% among men and 44% among women. 15% of the women had 4 or more live births. As high as 68% women found it difficult to access health facilities. It was found that the general and reproductive health situation of the women in the tribal population was very poor. For example, women had high abortions ratio and infant mortality rates were also high according to the 1998-2003 figures. 54% of the women reported of some or the other form of gynaecological morbidity. 60% of the women had unmet need for contraception. 33% of the women did not use contraception because of the fear of the sideeffects, 24% did not use it as husband did not like it, while 26% reported that they did not use it as they wanted more children.

The tribals had low literacy with lower sex ratio showing low status of females within the tribal system and very low child sex ratio, which needed urgent attention from the researchers, planners and policy makers. The efforts at developing the physical conditions of tribals in the state were inadequate and problems such as shortage of water and difficulty in accessing medical care still persisted. The infant mortality and foetal wastage were also high among tribes along with a high proportion of reproductive morbidities among the women.

Women and Mental Health

Women were more prone to suffer from mental problems not because of their biology, but because of the multiple roles they had to perform. These coupled with lack of decision-making capacity, poor status at the household and community level, making them vulnerable to violence, sexual abuse, neglect, gender discrimination, poverty, hunger, malnutrition, overwork made women vulnerable to mental health problems.

Kerala had a very high suicide rate in the country with the figures of 29.6/100000, which was much higher than the average suicide rates for the country, which were 0.57/100000. Kerala reported of 27suicides per day and these took place among people in the age groups of 30-60 years. The reasons for suicides included financial problems, marital conflicts. Studies showed that suicides were high among the married as compared to unmarried. The male to female ratio for suicides in the state was 7:3. The gender difference in the state with respect to suicides was diminishing.

Depression was found to be increasing among women in the state. The solutions to the problems related to mental health in the state included increasing awareness among people to seek help at the earliest, counselling as well as social interventions. In addition to this, human rights issues of mentally ill patients also needed to be addressed.

Health Needs of Elderly Women

The health needs of the elderly included:

Medical, Social and Nursing needs. For example, in spite of the presence of one or more ailments, majority of the elderly are able to carry out their normal activities without assistance. Only in the last few years of the life span do ageing individuals need close assistance from family members. The physicians dealing with elderly patients not only have to deal with specific health problems, but also the social and the psychological health needs of the elderly.

Many of the health problems of elderly were essentially the result of non-medical factors. For example, stress and isolation, the result of the socio economic challenges were closely associated with disease and illness among the elderly. Family had to be considered as the most important and effective resource to the physician. Changes also needed to be made at the level of policy, education. Thus, there was need to include the care of elderly training into the syllabus of doctors, nurses and paramedics. Steps needed to be devised to help in early detection of ailments and under lying causes of ailments with follow up of treatment. Prevention means such as preventing falls could also be devised. Other than this, there was a need for devising simple effective screening programmes and providing equipments to the rural Health centres to help in early detection of problems among the elderly.

Overcoming manpower shortages in terms of training of non-physician personnel such as geriatric nurse social worker and other caregivers was necessary. The schools of nursing and social work needed to develop curriculum emphasising geriatric care. It was also necessary to overcome the legal and regulatory barriers to the use of services of non-physician personnel.

Health of Female Agricultural Workers in Kerala

Gender roles and frequent health problems restricted the women's attendance on available workdays. Women were not politically aware and this was reflected in that only few were able to name their trade union where they were members, many did not know anything about the union, while majority revealed that nothing had been conveyed to them regarding trade union activities except membership fees. It was found that women were not able to participate in political activities because of lack of opportunities than their own disinterest.

At the household level, majority of the women bore the burden of the household responsibilities without help from the men. They had poor decision-making capacity at the household level. Alcoholism among husbands, physical and sexual violence was a part of their everyday lives.

Women utilised the public health services in case of illness, but were found to be highly dissatisfied with the quality of treatment available. Many complained of corrupt practices such as acceptance of bribes at the health services. Spending on health care was the most important reason for indebtedness among the women.

At the Policy Level

There was a need to devise a health policy for Kerala that was based on Kerala's specific health problems. At present, Kerala had the same pattern of services as all other states, despite having a very different health profile.

Health equity had to be made an explicit goal in the health policy and allocations made to disadvantaged areas and groups, and under-served populations such as women of post-reproductive age groups also had to be based on equitable grounds.

Gender equity in health needed to be addressed as an explicit objective in all health programmes and interventions for health problems affecting both women and men

Special attention needed to be paid to the unfinished agenda and unaddressed agenda in reproductive health, as a part of gender equity goals. For example, gender-based violence as a public health issue and sexual health issues needed urgent attention.

The 'Right to Health' had to be acknowledged in health policy and the state's obligation for promoting accessibility, availability, affordability and quality had to be acknowledged.

Private sector had to be appropriately regulated and harnessed to serve the state's health-policy goals of equity in health.

Health services needed to be 'transparent' and 'accountable' to citizens in accordance with the rights-based approach (For example, maternal death audits could be made public information). Mechanisms had to be developed for enforcing accountability, for e.g. through patient advocates, regular NHRC hearings or similar mechanisms for complaints and redressal.

At the Programme Level

A social and gender audit of health programmes and health service delivery at various levels could be done. For example, questions like "How well did they serve the goals of social and gender equity? What needed to be done to improve the quality of the programme?" needed to be asked. For example, there were several interventions to make programmes and services responsive to gender-based causes, underlying health problems and gender-barriers in accessing services.

There was a need to carry out gender and rights training of health programme managers, health service providers at various levels.

There was a need to address the gender issues present within the health system such as problems faced by women health providers.

There was a need to conduct pre service training of health providers through integrating gender and social issues/rights-approach in teaching and clinical training for medical professionals, nursing and paramedical trainees.

At the Level of the Research Community

There was a need to undertake research on a wide range of health and gender equity issues in different settings.

There was a need to identify new areas for 'activist' research such as monitoring health impact of development programmes and publicising these.

There was a need for a different approach to research. There was a need to do research that followed the bottom-up approach; that which gave voice to lived experiences; that which was collaborative and multidisciplinary across different groups working on health and related issues.

There was a need to play a leadership role in developing policy and programme alternatives through participatory processes.

At the Level of the Panchayati Raj Institutions

Training on gender and rights issues in health could be imparted to office bearers responsible for decision-making as well as to women and men leaders.

Steps could be taken to ensure allocation of resources for addressing specific health issues affecting women in women's component plans. Workshops/screening camps/health festivals etc. could be organised in collaboration with local PHCs (e.g. for newly married couples on issues related to gender, sexuality and reproductive health).

At the level of Women's Groups, NGOs, Activists and Civil Society Organisations

There was a need to increase awareness regarding gender and health equity and rights issues among women and men and among decision-makers.

There was a need to increase informed participation in policy debates and policy formulation.

There was a need to actively involve organised groups of women such as SHGs through training and opportunities for participation in the above.

There was a need to insist on the state's obligation to meet the health care needs of the people through adequate investment in the public sector and regulation of the private sector.

There was a need to hold health services accountable to violation of health rights. This could be done in an informed and systematic way, e.g. through participation in hospital and PHC review committees and not through sporadic and reactive protest actions.

5

Rural Women and Employment

Women have always formed an integral part of the labour force especially in rural areas and have played an important role in sustaining the economy. Studies have shown that the earnings of adult women are proportionally more important in poor than in better-off families. Women's work throughout the country is more affected by the family situation than men's. The household structure as well as the sex distribution of labour and resources affect women's economic behaviour. Marital status and the number and age of children are also powerful determinants of women's economic participation.

Incomes are generated through production and received in the form of wages and salaries, operating surpluses of enterprises, incomes of self-employment, and the value of production by households for their own consumption. Of course, from an economic perspective, incomes also include property revenues such as interest, dividend, royalty and rent. Value added generated in the household sector, as it has come to be known, includes unpaid work like housekeeping, child-care, cooking, nursing the sick and elderly, vegetable gardening, do-it-yourself activities, and so on. Such activities do not have a market price.

The services of housewives are similar to those of farmers who consume part of their produce and therefore should be counted as a contribution to the household sector. Thus, strategic issues for helping women include improving productivity of small farms; income generation through micro-enterprises; human capital formation, and removing general and institutional barriers that prevent women from become initiators and beneficiaries of economic development.

A major cost was an increase in unemployment among low-income women who previously hand-pounded the crop, while benefits were in the form of lower consumer prices and increased incomes for rice millers. The needs of rural women range from drinking water, natural gas, electricity, sanitary facilities, kindergartens, basic health care, vocational training and basic education to decent shelter, low-cost transportation, employment programmes, and credit for small businesses. It is fundamental not only to increase the access of rural women to services for a decent life in the villages, but also to expand services that will help women to contribute more to the growth of the rural economy.

Local government action should include:

— Infrastructure development for transportation, sanitation, public safety, recreation and health;

— Encouraging informal sector involvement in housing, transportation, sanitation, security, education, health and recreation; and

— Establishment of employment centres in low-income districts to recruit women for non-farm enterprises.

FEMALE PARTICIPATION IN AGRICULTURAL PRODUCTION

Rural Indian women are extensively involved in agricultural activities. However, the nature and extent of their involvement differs with the variations in agro-production systems. The mode of female participation in agricultural production varies with the land-owning status of farm households. Their roles range from managers to landless labourers. In overall farm production, women's average contribution is estimated at 55 per cent to 66 per cent of the total labour with percentages much higher in certain regions.

In the Indian Himalayas a pair of bullocks works 1064 hours, a man 1212 hours and a woman 3485 hours in a year on a one-hectare farm, a figure which illustrates women's significant contribution to agricultural production. Women provide one half of the labour in rice cultivation in India. In the plantation sector women are the crucial labourers. Depending on the region and crops, women's contributions vary but they provide pivotal labour from planting to harvesting and post-harvest operations. Traditionally, women had usufruct rights to the community land. But after the land reforms, land titles were given to men, denying women's access to land.

Role of Crop Production

India has a variety of crops grown in irrigated and rainfed areas. Rice, wheat, jowar, maize and bajra are the major foodgrains. Oilseed, sugarcane, cotton and jute are the important cash crops. Likewise, tea and coffee are important plantation crops. India's agricultural production systems also include a wide range of horticultural crops.

Rice is widely grown in Southern, Eastern and Northeastern states. Wheat is mainly grown in Punjab and Haryana. Jowar and Bajra are important foodgrains in dryland areas. Assam and West Bengal are famous for tea, whereas Karnataka, Tamil Nadu and Kerala are coffee and coconut producing states.

In the highly diversified Indian context, no simple gender division of labour exists with regard to crop production. In certain areas in India women play a key role as seed selectors and in seedling production. Their knowledge on seeds and seed storage contribute to the viability of the agricultural diversity and production. As weeders, women contribute to crop management. Women prepare and apply green and farm-yard manure. As integrated pest management practices are introduced, it could be expected that women's work will increase due to more labour-intensive activities.

Role of Livestock Production

In India, livestock plays a multifaceted role in providing draught power for the farm, manure for crops, energy for cooking and food for household consumption as well as the market. In animal husbandry women have a multiple role. With regional difference, women take care of animal production. Their activities vary widely ranging from care of animals, grazing, fodder collection, cleaning of animal sheds to processing milk and livestock products. In livestock management, indoor jobs like milking, feeding, cleaning, etc. are done by women in 90 per cent of families while management of male animals and fodder production are effected by men.

Women accounted for 93 per cent of total employment in dairy production. Depending upon the economic status, women perform the tasks of collecting fodder, collecting and processing dung. Dung composting and carrying to the fields is undertaken by women. Women also prepare cooking fuel by mixing dung with twigs and crop residues. Though women play a significant role in livestock management and production, women's control over livestock and its products is negligible. The vast majority of the dairy cooperative membership is assumed by men, leaving only 14 per cent to women.

Women and Forestry

The Indian population, particularly the rural, is highly dependent upon forests. Fuelwood contributes 84 per cent of the total household energy consumption. There are 66.5 million tribals in India and with few exception, the majority of them are forest dwellers. Unfortunately, forests are deteriorating massively due to encroachment of agricultural production, mining, construction of dams, industrial and railway demand. The country has been loosing 1.5 million hectares of forest cover annually. In India about 16 per cent of the total geographical area is covered by woodland and forests. Gender roles in using forest resources vary widely depending upon the region as well as socio-economic class and tribal affiliation.

Rural Indian women's interface with the forests is varying — gathering, wage employment, production in farm forestry and management of afforested areas in the community plantation. In India, women are the major gatherers and users of a much more diverse range of forest products than men. Depending upon the socio-cultural variations among different communities, primarily Non-timber Forest Products (NTFP) are collected by women and timber by men. In several parts of India, large proportions of the population depend on NTFP as their main source of livelihood.

Apart from fodder and fuel, women collect food, medicinal plants, building materials, material for household items and farm implements. Sal and Tendu leaves are primarily collected by women. As women are the ones who have traditionally been collecting forest products, they posses the knowledge of properties and potential uses of these products.

Women in Fisheries

India is among the top ten fish producing countries in the world contributing about 3 per cent to the world marine fish catch. About 5 million people in the coastal areas carry out fishing and allied activities for their livelihood. In India, nature and extent of women's participation in fishery varies across the states. Fish drying/curing, marketing, and handbraiding and net-mending are the main areas of women's involvement in Tamil Nadu, Andhra Pradesh and Orissa. Women are also involved in shrimp processing in these states. In addition, in Andhra Pradesh, women are engaged in mollusc and shell collection on a seasonal basis in a few places along the coastline. However, marine fish capture is a men's domain.

Among the mangroves of Bhitarkanika on the Orissa coast, both women and men fish in the fresh water estuarine areas. Men cast nets while women and children catch fish with hands. But fishing by boat in the flood tides is exclusively performed by men. In contrast, women's participation in small-scale fisheries is very limited in West Bengal. Even ancillary industry, which in the other Indian east coast states is a women's domain, is dominated by men, as a relatively low number of days in a year is spent on actual fishing. In the fishing villages, fish drying/curing is performed by both women or men who do not belong to the fishing community. In coastal aquaculture, women are involved in prawn and seed collection to a very limited extent.

EXTENSION ACTIVITIES

The centre organised 2 trainers' training programmes for the benefit of 22 beneficiaries. Forty-nine trainings for farm women were organised through which 1,850 farm women were benefited in value addition, organic farming, nutrition and gardening. In addition one Kisan Mela was also organised for the 150 farm women. On this occasion exhibition, *mahila goshti* and quiz were organised. Six radio talks were also delivered by the scientists.

Krishi Vigyan Kendra (KVK)

The KVKs organised 28,544 training programmes for 1.97 lakh farm women, rural girls and women extension personnel including 64,601 SC/ST beneficiaries. The KVKs have organised 6,576 extension programmes including field days, kisan melas, exhibitions, exposure visits etc., in which 73,152 farm women participated.

Self-Help Groups of Women (SHG)

Self help groups (SHG) were formed by KVK Gadag with 2,167 members from 5 blocks. It has also conducted training programmes for the members on concept of SHG and thrift besides arranging exposure visits to successful SHGs. The thrift and credit activities of the SHGs include Rs 28.50 lakh savings by the SHGs during the year and Internal lending of Rs 22.00 lakh to the members. Twenty-six training programmes on various income generating activities were conducted by the KVK for 599 SHG members. Many of the SHGs were linked to the financial institutions and other government agencies for financial assistance. The total revolving fund of the groups was Rs 66.38 lakh.

The income generating activities taken up by the SHGs included home made products, bakery products, small business, tailoring/embroidery, goat/buffalo rearing and vermicomposting.

Innovative marketing outlets for SHGs: The KVK initiated the concept of Saturday Bazar in Gadag town to encourage the SHG members by providing suitable market outlet. The farmers and farmwomen belonging to SHG groups only were allowed to sell the goods in Saturday bazaar after they undergo training at the KVK and the KVK home scientist verifies the quality of their products. They were also issued identity cards by the KVK. The products in the market included fresh fruits, vegetables, pickles, crisp rotis of jowar, and bajra. On an average 50 SHG members participated in the bazaar every week and the weekly transaction of the bazaar varied from Rs 15,000-20,000. Based on the consumer demand another market, Sunday Bazaar was started by the KVK at another place. Currently the KVK is performing role of a facilitator to ensure smooth running of the markets.

Women in Cyber Extension: The KVK, Ahmednagar, Maharashtra, with the support of the host organisation established high-speed computer network linking its ten institutions through wireless radio frequency and the institutions located within 5 km radius with a wide area network (WAN). The Krishi Vigyan Kendra apart from having the Internet access from the Pravara Network and internal network linking all the Subject Matter Specialists (SMS) with all the villages in the network had access to internet as well. All the SMSs of the KVK frequently build up the information repository for agriculture extension at its server, which is available for all those connected to the wireless LAN in the Pravara Network.

The local website in the wide area network provides textual information on 17 important fruits, 16 vegetables, 6 flowers, 5 improved technologies, 6 soil related problems, one IPM, 16 field crops and one on processing. Apart from this the KVK has also prepared visual material accessible for the farmers that comprises 14-multi-media presentation and one audio presentation called Tomato Extension and Training Information System. The information that is required by the farmers has been compiled specifically in Marathi for the farmers to facilitate easy understanding of the improved crop cultivation practices related to various crops grown by them. In all 646 women farmers from 4 villages availed the facilities of IT Centres for information which include 246 for technology, 98 for market information, 33 for weather and 269 for other information.

Production of vermiculture: The Andhra Pradesh Mahila Samatha Society, Karimnagar and Adilabad district has started their Samatha Dharani Programme, which is a joint farming programme of food crops by the SC, ST and weaker section women. The programme envisages production of food crops through safe methods of agriculture. Earthworms (4 kg) of mixed culture were supplied to these women beneficiaries and established units at Godishala, Husnabad, Potharam and Bejjanki; 100 women started the project and produced 128 tonnes of vermicompost.

AICRP on Home Science for Women's Empowerment

An important component of empowerment in Third World Countries comprises rural women who play multiple crucial roles in all spheres of development activities. In the recent past added emphasis has been laid on acknowledging and preparing database on multidimensional role sets of women where their roles have become an inbuilt factor for input-output system of empowerment. In this process, the All India Coordinated Research Project (AICRP) on Home Science aims at developing resource base of rural women for empowering them to become subsistence-generating units for sustaining development and improving quality of life.

At the initial stage of the project, the prescriptive approach was used which dealt with exploring information for providing a package of instruction regarding what rural women should do to endure health security, food security, economic security and livelihood security. Gradually the project thrust shifted towards integrated and participatory approaches for working with rural women in their own context. For this, the nutrition component laid emphasis on nutritional security for human health in agrarian ecosystem.

The component focused attention on documenting uncommon foods for its wider acceptability by determining nutritional quality of identified food sources, development of recipes and nutrition guide. The nutrition guide is user-friendly computer software for knowledge empowerment of nutrition educators and its subsequent transfer at grassroot level.

The nutrition component has also strived to identify micro-nutrient deficiencies with the aim to suggest diet modifications and establish nutrition gardens as approaches to health and nutrition security. The Human Development component which initially focused attention on data generation for developing growth norms of rural children is now empowering rural mothers for optimal development of children through interventions on scientific child care practices.

The establishments of farm creche for comprehensive child care facilities in supplementary feeding and development of child through creative play materials. The training of creche workers through training materials on child care practices empowers them to be efficient caretakers.

The ergonomic management of drudgery undertaken by Family Resource Management component aims at introducing women-friendly drudgery reducing technologies related to farm, home and allied activities. The ergonomic cost is being calculated for respective tool/technology as a measure for suggesting improvements in tool/technology that will promote health empowerment.

The clothing and textile component since its inception has focused attention on economic feasibility of use of locally available agro and animal based fibres and exploration of indigenous dyes textile product preparation. A large wealth of natural dyes has been explored for use on wool and silk and the interventions have been conducted to empower rural women and weavers with knowledge and skill. The economic empowerment is also being assured by transferring technologies of natural dyes to rural women for preparing textile handicrafts.

The database on rural women and indigenous knowledge being undertaken by Extension component has suggested several pathways for empowerment of rural women with reference to their participation and decision-making roles in farming and allied activities as per indicators of qualitative data.

The pathways have highlighted on empowerment of knowledge, skill, decision-making; economic and social empowerment. The data base on indigenous knowledge has strongly suggested for empowering women with knowledge on locally available plant sources for ensuring health security.

NEW EMPLOYMENT OPPORTUNITIES

The North-Eastern Region of India, comprising the states of Arunachal Pradesh, Assam, Manipur, Meghalaya, Mizoram, Nagaland, Sikkim and Tripura, has a total cropped area of 5.3 million hectares and a population of around 39 million. The region falls under high rainfall zone and the climate ranges from subtropical to alpine. The region is characterised by difficult terrain, wide variations in slopes, altitude, land tenure systems and diverse cultivation practices.

Table 5.1. Male and Female Rural Farm Employment in the North-East (except Sikkim)

India/N.E/ NE states	*Male (M) Female (F)*	*Percentage Share 1981*	*1991*	*2001*
All India	M	81.70	79.70	68.34
	F	89.10	89.55	77.05
North–east	M	75.66	70.49	59.32
	F	89.25	75.04	66.53
Arunachal	M	67.98	59.80	62.58
	F	96.10	91.65	86.73
Assam	M	NA	70.91	58.51
	F	NA	66.29	60.87
Manipur	M	77.82	62.40	59.33
	F	77.72	80.00	63.68
Meghalaya	M	86.92	74.50	72.37
	F	87.89	84.08	80.79
Mizoram	M	77.32	75.68	79.33
	F	95.95	93.89	90.99
Nagaland	M	69.73	74.26	89.85
	F	96.64	93.10	86.56
Tripura	M	75.70	69.12	55.06
	F	83.12	77.81	69.53

The transport and communication system is poorly developed and as a result majority of the areas in the region remain still inaccessible. The infrastructure facilities like supply of input, marketing, institutional credit and extension services are inadequate. Majority of the population, predominantly tribal, is dependent on agriculture and land-based activities. The agricultural production system in the region is predominantly rain-fed, mono-cropped at subsistence level. Slash and burn agriculture is still practiced in almost all the states except Sikkim on steep slopes with reduced cycle of 2 to 3 years as against 10-15 years in the past. Sixty seven percentages of its total main women workers depend on agriculture for their livelihood (Table 5.1).

This of course, varies from state to state. States like Mizoram, Nagaland, Meghalaya and Arunachal Pradesh have very high percentage of woman workers (higher than the national average) engaged in agriculture.

Agriculture is the main economic activity in the region and despite major impact of green revolution in the irrigated areas of the country; modernisation of agriculture has escaped this region. The agricultural practices in the region are broadly of two types, viz., (i) settled farming practiced in the plains, valleys, and foothills and (ii) shifting cultivation practiced on the hill slopes. The region's agriculture is characterised by low crop intensity (117 per cent).

Context of New Employment Opportunities

The 'contexts' are the ideological, political, social, economic, technological, and institutional frameworks at the level of the household or community or region that create and shape work avenues for women in agriculture in a region.

Increased access to education and health

Literacy rate for women has increased in the north-east (58 per cent as per 2001 census). This has had and will have its positive impact on the ideological, political and social planes in the household and community in terms of influencing the power relations. Along with better health, educational advancement shall increase the bargaining power of woman to claim ownership to land, credit and other assets etc., besides becoming an active partner in household and community decision-making process.

All this may happen through the positive changes that education and training are having and will have on the mindset, faiths and beliefs of both men and women. This is expanding and will expand women's mobility, their control over labour, produce and income, exercise of political power and participation in household and community decision-making process.

Infrastructure development

Over the last two and half decades, the quantity and quality of economic and institutional infrastructures in the NE region has got expanded and presently the central government is concentrating more on this. These developments have happened and are going to happen in the fields of physical transportation, electronic and telecommunications, irrigation, power, banking and insurance services. These developments are helping women in agriculture to move from subsistence agriculture to productive agriculture.

NGOs and formation of SHGs

Involvement of a good number of NGOs and formation of SHGs, that educate and train women in matters of participation in economic activities including agriculture, makes women more enterprising and reassuring. Development NGOs directly create job avenues for the woman folk in agriculture and allied sectors particularly in rural areas by creating new quality job avenues and expanding the value addition chain.

Recently some of the NGOs are trying to integrate a gender perspective in the programmes that they undertake. These NGOs along with some government organisations are adopting a combination of three strategies to effectively empower women and create work opportunities for them. These strategies are:

- — Advocacy strategies which aim at changes in the policy, legislation, resource allocation patterns and practices of different intergovernmental organisations,
- — Capacity building strategies which enhance women's ability to claim their due share of resources and power both in their families, communities *vis-a-vis* the market place and government organisations,
- — organisational strategies which help women to gain control over their self and economic, social, and political resources.

The emergence of SHGs is strengthening women's bargaining power in the community and their resolve to stand on their own feet.

Emergence of new institutes

Setting up of new and/or revamping the existing institutes of research, extension, training, finance and marketing in the NER is going to have its impact on women's participation in agriculture. Institutes like IIT, bamboo institute, spice board, institutes of technology in various universities, agricultural universities, branches of ICAR, National Research Centre on Mithun, National Research Centre on Yak, National Research Centre on orchid, Krishi Vigyan Kendras, KVIC etc. are going to provide much needed research and extension services in agriculture. Institutes like NABARD, commercial banks, microcredit organisations are meeting the financial needs of the women farmers. Many of these institutes have been sensitised about gender perspectives in their research and activities. Significant fallout of these research activities in the form of new and appropriate technology, is benefiting and shall benefit women in agriculture.

Government initiative

Government initiative in the form of women friendly legislation enabling women to have access to parental agricultural properties, weather forecasting, providing facilities such as agri-marketing, agri-extension, agri-finance, agri-insurance etc. do have their impact on women's participation in agriculture.

Political empowerment

Positive changes in the form of reservation of seats in grassroot democratic institutions is directly empowering the rural women in terms of community decision-making.

Globalisation, liberalisation, look-east policy and WTO

Globalisation has brought in new changes in the economic field which directly and indirectly influence women's participation in agriculture. Globalisation in theory, provides an opportunity for women in developing countries to produce for the global market. In a globalised world, the taste and preferences of the consumers change fast. Demand for environment friendly technology also increases. However, as the market becomes global, it is supposed to create enough opportunities of work for women in agriculture in terms of producing varieties of products on commercial basis.

Under liberalisation, as restriction on movement of produce eases, as information reaches everywhere on the click of a mouse, as capital and labour flow freely among regions and as inspector raj goes off; the market size for agricultural and agro-processed commodities gets enlarged.

Further, under the look-east policy, Government of India has an ambitious plan to integrate the markets of the North-East India with that of the South-East and East-

Asian Countries including Bangladesh. Once this policy becomes viable and operational, it is expected that this would create employment opportunities for women in the farm and allied sectors of the economy of the northeastern region.

In the field of agriculture, the objective of WTO is to reform trade in agricultural commodities and make it more market oriented. Thus, theoretically, it looks that it would create substantial job opportunities for women in agriculture in developing countries in terms of having more market access in the developing countries because of reduction in export and domestic subsidies by the developed countries. However, this is subject to a lot of conditions and would be a long-term proposition.

Farm, non-farm linkage and diversification of employment

A rapid development in infrastructure, development of new and appropriate technology, provision of expanded extension services, social, political and economic empowerment of women and spread of NGO network to rural areas; all these developments help in increasing productivity in agriculture, ensuring food security and environmental sustainability. Hence, subsistence agriculture gives space to commercial or productive agriculture. As a result of which, increased diversification of employment happens in the economy in the form of farm and non-farm sector linkage. This has its obvious positive implications for female employment in agriculture and allied sectors particularly in the rural areas.

Women friendly society

Although the status of women in N.E. society varies across communities, still in general their average social position is better than that of the women in the mainland of India. Meghalaya society is matrilineal. Other northeastern societies, in different states, are ideologically more empowered than the societies in the mainland India.

WOMEN IN INFORMAL EMPLOYMENT

Almost all the employment in developed economies is created within the recognised institutional framework as the economic agents which create these jobs operate within the existing laws and regulation. These economic agents are the government, and private enterprises, including non-corporate entities, and the employment thus created is governed by the prevailing labour laws and regulations.

In contrast, in the developing countries the vast majority of the population is left to fend for itself and create employment out of its own ingenuity, skills and capital. This leads to vast differences in the nature of employment and the creation of a dualistic structure of "formal" and "informal" components of the labour market.

The reasons for the growth of the informal sector are important from the point of view of developing policies. Whatever the reason, the growth of the informal sector in the emerging labour market is inevitable. Women's employment in the informal sector is also likely to rise due to various reasons. With the adoption of the structural adjustment programme women tend to loose ground in the formal sectors of the economy. The growth of ancillarisation and industrial employment through subcontracting appears to be gaining importance.

Stagnating and falling incomes of households due to poor performance of the economy also leads to increased entry of women into the labour market. The process of globalisation, export-oriented industrialisation and relocation of industries from the developed to the developing countries also lead to the increase in the employment in the informal sector. Women's employment is often favoured in many of these industries.

Process of Informalisation

In the developing countries the process of informalisation of the labour force takes place broadly in two ways. Work is pushed out of the factories and formal work situations into small workshops (sweatshops), the homes and informal situations. That is, there is an international trend in subcontracting of work and a consequent increase in informal work, often in homeworking. Secondly, the workers who remain in the factories or in formal work situations, are governed by looser contracts and obtain fewer social security benefits. That is, there is an attempt on the part of the employer to reduce his liabilities.

Components of the Informal Economy

The informal sector distinguishes two kinds of enterprises, namely, own account enterprises and enterprises of informal employers. The activity status of employment is the closest that this enterprise based definition can get to distinguishing the informal economy. The present activity status classification of the International Classification of Status in Employment (ICSE), ILO consists of the following categories: employees, employers, own account workers, members of producer's co-operatives, contributing family members, workers not classifiable by status.

Workers in the informal economy can be broadly distinguished into wage employment and non-wage employment, each consisting of the following components:

Non-wage Employment

- — Own account workers;
- — Employers/owners of informal enterprises with at least one hired worker;
- — Unpaid family helpers in both types of informal enterprises.

Wage Employment

- — Employees in the enterprises of informal employers;
- — Outworkers or Homeworkers: persons working at home, or on premises of his choice other than the employer's, to produce goods or services on a contract or order for a specific employer or contractor;
- — Independent wage workers not attached to only one employer, and providing services to individuals, households and enterprises, e.g., maid servants and watchmen working for households.
- — Informal employment in formal sector enterprises: workers whose pay and benefits do not conform to existing labour regulations.

This categorisation is similar to that developed by Sethuraman. In the literature the first four categories above are generally taken to represent employment in the informal sector. The need to distinguish the category of independent wage workers can be debated. In many Latin American countries domestic servants are distinguished in the national surveys and together with independent wage workers are added to the informal sector.

The first process of informalisation of the labour force, pushing work out of formal work situations, leads to an increase in the first component, non-wage employment. It can also lead to increase in the first two varieties of the second component, i.e., informal wage employment. The second process of informalisation, resulting in looser contracts and fewer benefits, leads to an increase in the last category of workers, informal employment within the formal enterprises as defined by the enterprise-based approach.

Measure of the non-wage employment

Obviously it is not easy to obtain empirical estimates of these categories of workers from the national official labour statistics. However, we can arrive at an approximation of the first component of the informal economy, non-wage employment or self-employment, by the addition of employers, own account workers and unpaid family helpers in the activity status classification of the national labour force survey.

While it may be relatively safe to assume that own account workers and unpaid family helpers are part of the informal economy, this assumption may not be very accurate for the category of employer. Employers, however, form a very small proportion of the workforce.

Measure of the wage employment

The second component of the informal economy is even more difficult to demarcate from the official data since there is really a continuum in the degree of informality in the employer-employee relationships. The official data distinguish only employees.

The Indian labour force surveys further classifies them into casual and regular. All regular workers do not necessarily belong to the formal economy, as they often do not receive a variety of benefits due to the formal worker such as provident funds, paid leave etc.

Non-Agricultural Sector

The closest one can come to distinguishing the two components of the informal economy from the population census and labour force surveys is by using the activity status classification. These data divided into five countries. Almost the whole of the agricultural sector can be considered to be informal. Any measure of the informal economy including the agricultural sector would indicate a decline.

Hence a good measure of changes in the informal economy over time would perhaps be to concentrate on the non-agricultural sector. A rough estimate of the informal economy in the non-agricultural sector is obtained as the proportion of the non-wage workers, self-employed and unpaid family workers, to total workers in this sector. This constitutes what we earlier distinguished as the first component of the informal economy. The non-agricultural sector is disaggregated into the secondary and tertiary sectors, with the tertiary sector being split further into trade and services.

The first component of the informal sector, non-wage workers in the non-agricultural work force, was most predominant in Bangladesh followed by Pakistan and India. It was the least important component in Sri Lanka. This was true for women workers as well.

The trends in the changes in the first component of the informal economy were rather mixed in the South Asian countries. An increase in the non-wage component in employment was observed clearly in India and Bangladesh.

6

Socio-economic Development of Rural Women

The development process in India as envisaged by the Five-Year Plans was to be geared to an equal share for women in development. Development for and the welfare of woman received particular attention from the beginning of the planning process. Women were provided special attention in three sectors—education, social welfare, and health. At the same time, a proactive role for women was envisaged. The Central Social Welfare Board encouraged women's organisations, especially at the grassroots, to promote welfare measure in partnership with the government, with mahila mandals conceived as delivery mechanisms. Thus, '... there was a conceptual thrusts towards actively involving and stimulating the participation of women's organisations in the processes of change'.

FIRST PLAN

The First Plan focused on women's legitimate role in the family and in the community and emphasised the need for adequate welfare services. A well-organised social service department was set-up to look after women and child welfare. The Plan suggested the following measures:

— An advisory committee to be set-up by the Central Government to make proposals and review progress in respect of law and policy in different States.

— Enforcement of the law to be effectively carried out. Measures to enforce the law to include, wherever necessary, the creation of a separate vigilance branch within the police force.

— Adequate arrangements to be made for medical assistance.

— Wherever it was found that clandestine prostitution was in existence, efforts to be made to eradicate it.

— More institutions to be organised by local bodies and private social service agencies.

— Homes providing shelter, medical aid and assistance for marriage to function under the management of trained personnel and be subject to regulation, inspection and control.

— Strengthening of existing specialised and private agencies like vigilance associations and societies for the prevention of traffic in women.

SECOND PLAN

The Second Plan (1956-61) retained the welfare approach to women's issues, together with an appreciation of the need to organise women workers. The Plan took cognisance of the plight of the women workers on account of social prejudices/disabilities, as also the need to provide maternity benefits to them, protect women from injurious work, and set-up creches for their children. It was recognised that the equal pay for equal work policy required speedy implementation, together with the provision of training, to enable women compete for higher jobs.

THIRD PLAN

The Third Plan (1961-66) envisaged female education as a major strategy of welfare. Under 'social welfare', the emphasis was on the provision of rural welfare services and condensed educational courses. Health services were geared to maternal and child welfare, and also, health education, nutrition and family planning.

FOURTH PLAN

The Fourth Plan (1969-74) emphasised women's education and the promotion of women's welfare within the family. To bring down the birth rate, spending on family planning was increased. The plan agenda extended also to the immunisation of preschool children, and the supplementary feeding of children and of expectant and nursing mothers.

FIFTH PLAN

The Fifth Plan (1974-79) marked a shift in the approach towards women from 'wel fare' to 'development', with the scope of social welfare expanding to cope with the problems of the family and the role of women. The new approach was one of integrating welfare with developmental services.

The first plan recognised the problems of high infant and maternal mortality as primarily due to malnutrition, and thus undertook to develop school-feeding schemes in the State Public Health Departments and Maternity and Child Health Centres. Though important in their own spheres, the programmes centred on welfare measures for women in the context of their traditional role in the family.

The welfare approach to women continued into the Second Plan, which also took cognisance of the condition of women workers, not only as a comparatively less organised category, but also, as a vulnerable one, in view of the social prejudices and physical disabilities suffered by them. Women were to be protected against injurious work and receive maternity benefits, and creches for their children were to be set up. Speedy implementation of equal pay for equal work was suggested, together with the provision for training to enable women compete for higher jobs and expand opportunities for part-time employment.

In the early years of planning, the assumption was that women would automatically benefit from the overall measures for national development. In the initial development plans, women were, for the main part, the 'passive beneficiaries' of welfare programmes. In the seventies, winds of change began to below. In 1975, the Committee on the Status of women in India comprehensively assessed women's problems in terms of its social, economic, legislative and political dimensions and made several recommendations to secure social justice for women, remove obstacles to their advancement, and provide them opportunities so that they could realise their potential to the full.

The International Women's Year and the International Women's Decade too provided a significant thrust to the changes in policy towards women's issues. Efforts were directed towards the formulation of alternative strategies for women's development and an information system for monitoring and evaluating progress. The capacity of the administration to better plan and administer women's development programmes and the need to strengthen it too received emphasis.

SIXTH PLAN

The Sixth Plan (1980-85) 'for the first time in India's

planning history' included 'a chapter on women and development'. This was an important step towards planning for women's development. Indian women were perceived no longer as subjects for welfare, they were seen as active partners in development. Women's development needs as well as numbers of beneficiaries were identified for several beneficiary oriented programmes. A National Perspective Plan for women was prepared. Special institutions for women's development were established, among them, the National Committee on Women under the Chairmanship of the Prime Minister. A separate Bureau of Women's Development was set-up by the Department of Social Welfare, followed by the creation of a separate Department of Women and Child Development and the setting up of special cells to deal with women's issues in different sectors.

Finally, the National Commission for Women Act of 1990 provided for the setting up of a commission with a wide range of functions for safeguarding women's rights, guiding their socio-economic development and evaluating the measures taken for women's development.

SEVENTH PLAN

The Seventh Plan (1985-90) continued with the approach of development programmes for women with the objective of raising their socio-economic status and bringing them into the mainstream of national development. Beneficiary-oriented programmes were promoted with the purpose of extending direct benefits to women. However, in identifying concrete strategies, there was a tendency to slide back into women-specific sectors and a refusal to extend the quota or the special component Plan approach'. Still, ' ... the Department of Rural Development announced a 30 per cent quota for women in all anti-poverty programmes in rural areas, in addition to the women-specific experimental programme introduced midway through the Sixth Plan.

EIGHTH PLAN

The Eighth Plan (1992-97) sought to ensure that women were not bypassed in access to the benefits of development from the different sectors. Special programmes were to be implemented to enrich the existing development programmes, and benefits to women in the sectors of education, health, and employment were to be monitored. Women were to be equal partners in the development process. The approach shifted from women's development to women's empowerment.

Together with the inequity in the labour market, the situation of women is characterised by gender difference in access to land, productive resources, information, skills and education. For poor households, women's capacity to work, her health, and her knowledge are vital for survival. Statistics show that the labour force participation of women and their proportional contribution to the total family income are the highest in households with the lowest economic status. Thus, the poorest families are the most dependent on women's economic productivity. As the percentage of women in extreme poverty is estimated to be large, reservations have been made in favour of women in the major poverty alleviation programmes:

— *IRDP* - the initial 10 per cent reservation for women in 1985-86 was increased to 34 per cent in 1993-94.

— *TRYSEM*-this programme has 40 per cent reservation for women. Till 1995, over 14,22,000 women benefited from this programme.

— *JRY*-the share of women till 1995 was 1035.93 million person days i.e., of the total employment generated under the programme, 24.19 per cent went in favour of women.

— *Indira Awas Yojana (IAY)*-Under this programme, dwelling units were allotted to women or were allotted in joint names with women, so that women could own assets.

— *DWCRA* (Development of Women and Children in Rural Areas): This programme has been in operation since 1982-83. Around 18000 groups constituted of women below the poverty line have been formed to take up economic activities to enhance their income generating capabilities and to improve their quality of life.

— Since 1986-87, Women's Development Corporations, constituted by the States, have made efforts to help women entrepreneurs and women co-operatives.

— *NABARD* (National Bank of Agriculture and Rural Development) - schemes relating to Priority Sector Lending (PSL) have been in operation and formation of Self Help Groups (SHGs) have been encouraged to make small credit available to women. Currently 2000 SHGs are in operation, of which women run 90 per cent.

— *SEWA* (Self-Employed Women's Association), seeks to reach out to poor-illiterate, self-employed women through the formation of women's co-operatives. The thirty thousand women members of SEWA include vendors and traders, home based skilled and semi-skilled workers and service providers in rural and urban sectors, who have formed their own co-operatives.

To combat the problem of poverty among women in urban areas, the Urban Basic Services Programme (UBSP) under the Nehru Rozgar Yojana (NRY) has been formulated. 30 per cent of the beneficiaries are women, whom the UBSP seeks to empower and actively involve in the planning and implementation of community development activities. Over 33,000 women, called Resident Community Volunteers (RVC), devote time in their own neighbourhood towards overall community development. Many of these volunteers are very poor, apart from being illiterate or semiliterate. In urban areas, women also benefit from thrift and credit societies, which are rapidly expanding.

NINTH PLAN

The Ninth Five-Year Plan (1997-2002) sets the objective of developing society on the basis of gender equality, women's empowerment and participation through gender mainstreaming in all sectors of national development. The main objectives of the Ninth Plan development policy are specified to involve women actively in various development fields, to increase women's access to political, economic, and social sectors, and to promulgate legal reforms to ensure women's equal legal rights. Equal participation of women is to be promoted by incorporating specific policies and programmes for women in sectoral development policies and plans. Special laws are promised for increasing women's participation at all levels of decision making, for establishing women's rights in landownership and for technical training in all fields. Initiatives to improve laws specially concern acts relating to land settlement, Legal Aid Act, compensation, partition of property, provisions of family law, compensation against torture Act.

The Ninth Plan intends to mainstream women into the planning process through training, education and promotion of women's groups. The focuses of this programme are skill promotion, income generation, empowerment, capacity building and employment creation etc.. There are some women focus education programmes such as alternative schooling, out of school programmes, incentive programmes for girls and disadvantaged children through formal and non-formal education. The Ninth plan includes also the assessment of women's contribution to household labour within the national accounting system; the development of gender-disaggregated indicators to measure women's participation in development and an effective co-ordination between agencies and bodies engaged in the field of women's development.

TENTH PLAN

The Tenth Plan (2002-2007) document identifies malnutrition, poor health, lack of education, overwork, violence and systemic powerlessness as markers of the life-long discrimination faced by women in India. The Tenth Plan represents a distinct advance from earlier plans, in terms of articulating a strong and time-bound platform for action on gender equality.

The Department of Women and Child Development (DWCD) is the national machinery for advancement of women. The Department formulates plans, policies and programmes, enacts/amends legislation and coordinates the efforts of both governmental and non-governmental organisations working on women's issues. The Department also implements innovative programmes for women and children. These programmes cover welfare and support services, training for employment and income generation, awareness generation and gender sensitisation. The National Policy and National Action Plan for Empowerment of Women have provided useful guidelines for the formulation of the project.

The Tenth Plan priorities related to women's equality and gender mainstreaming provide the broad framework for the present initiative. Specifically, the programme will focus on three strategies that have emerged as central to the overall approach to women's empowerment and gender equality in India. These strategies are:

— Enhancing participation of women in key institutions and decision-making structures at various levels.

— Strengthening the legal and regulatory framework for gender equality through bringing in legislation on women's rights in a range of sectors.

— Mainstreaming gender concerns in key national instruments of national policy, including national and state budgets, poverty alleviation policies and programmes, macro-economic policies and health policies.

The emphasis in the proposed programme will be on exploring some specific dimensions and impacts of these strategies. The total allocation for the project is USD 1 million.

ELEVENTH PLAN

The 11th Plan (2007-2012) must also pay special attention to gender equity and help create an enabling environment for the social, economic and political empowerment of women.The shameful practice of female foeticide, which is reflected in low and falling sex ratio for age group 0-6 must be stopped. The Plan focuses on ways of improving women's socio-economic status by mainstreaming gender quality concerns in all sectoral policies and programmes. Special efforts must be made to ensure that the benefits of government schemes accrue in appropriate proportions to women and girls.

Women in Panchayati Raj

The experience of women's global struggles shows that

the presence of a 'critical mass' of women within mainstream structures and institutions can kick-start the process of challenging and changing gender hierarchies within these structures and institutions, as well as energise and inspire larger processes of social change. The 73rd and 74th Constitutional Amendments, mandating one-third reservation of seats for women in local government, and the proposal to extend this provision to the Parliamentary level, are the most visible elements of this strategy.

While there are several studies in this field, particularly on women's presence within panchayati raj institutions, these have tended to focus on the role of individual women leaders rather than on the larger factors that enable or hamper the emergence of women's agenda, and the means by which they inspire and influence larger processes of social change. There are as yet few studies that systematically explore the dynamics of the change processes that result from initiatives to further women's participation and representation in social change processes.

It is therefore proposed to support a systematic analysis of the dynamics of women's engagement with panchayati raj institutions, and explore the factors that enable and constrain women's ability to take leadership of social change processes and bring a gender dimension into these processes. A total of 3-4 studies will be undertaken, and the findings collated to provide an assessment of the impact of women's enhanced presence in local-level political institutions on the overall status of women and on sectoral interventions.

Agencies for Women Belonging to Vulnerable Groups

There are numerous ongoing initiatives addressing the

concerns of the women belonging to the vulnerable groups, both by the government (notablyby the DWCD and the National Commission for Women) and also by other agencies. The Tenth Five Year Plan (2002-2007) suggests translating the National Policy for Empowerment of Women (2001) into action through Time Bound Plan. The first step in this direction is to draft a National Plan of Action for implementation of the policy by the DWCD. Owing to the heterogeneity of actors, approaches and actions, it is envisaged that a comprehensive mapping and collation exercise of the on going work especially with a focus on vulnerable groups (elderly women, women migrant and home-based workers, women with disabilities and women affected by HIV/AIDS) would provide insights in to the critical components of an effective policy design.

WTO Regime on Women Workers

A number of donors including UNDP, UNIFEM and the UN System as a whole have been involved in supporting initiatives in this regard. UNDP-supported State Human Development Reports and policy-influencing initiatives under other UNDP-supported programmes have yielded some valuable lessons. Persistent gender inequalities especially in the arena of work (both paid and unpaid) clearly point to the urgent need for understanding the dynamics of reforms. This need is further compounded by the likely gender differentiated impact of globalisation, liberalisation and new settings promoted by the WTO regime. In-depth studies to understand impact of structural adjustments, liberalisation and globalisation, WTO regime on women workers in collaboration with agencies like UNIFEM, UNCTAD etc. will be undertaken to provide inputs for a gender sensitive reform process.

COMMISSIONS AND COMMITTEES ON WOMEN'S EDUCATION

After Independence, the Government of India appointed several commissions and committees to look into women's education.

- *University Education Commission (1948-49)*: The University Education Commission recognised the need and importance of making educational opportunities available to women. It recommended that the ordinary amenities and decencies of life be provided for women in colleges, and advocated the development of women as both women and as citizens. Educational counselling was recommended to overcome prejudices against home-economics and home management, and women teachers were to be provided salaries on par with their male colleagues, on the principle of equal pay for equal work. The Commission also noted the necessity of separate schools for boys and girls in the 13-18 year age group.
- *Secondary Education Commission (1952-53)*: The Commission felt that there was no need to deal with women's education separately. In regard to co-education, there was considerable difference of opinion. The Commission suggested that separate schools for girls be established, wherever possible.
- *National Committee on Women's Education (1958-59)*: The Committee felt that State wise comprehensive development plans for girls should be conceived. Concessions for girls were recommended at the primary level, together with more co-educational institutions at the middle and secondary levels. Steps towards additional training institutions for women teachers in all areas was suggested, together with scholarships for girls to encourage

them to study traditionally male-dominated subjects like commerce, engineering and agriculture.

— *Committee on Differentiation of Curricula For Boys & Girls (1961)*: This committee emphasised that the traditional concepts of the inferiority of women be removed from the public mind.

— *Committee to Look Into the Causes for the Lack of Public Support, Particularly in Rural Areas, for Girls Education and to Enlist Public Co-Operation (1963)*: The Committee recommended concerted efforts to popularise girls education. It suggested school improvement conferences, attractive conditions of work for women teachers, involvement of local bodies in providing school buildings, equipment, playing fields, etc, literacy classes for women, and the provision of elective subjects of special interest to girls.

— *Education Commission (1964-66)*: The Commission reiterated the measures recommended by National Committee on Women's Education for accelerating the education of girls—provision of separate schools for girls, hostels and scholarships, part-time and vocational courses, increasing the scope for correspondence courses, employment of women teachers, and the setting up of research units in universities to deal with women's education.

— *Committee on the Status of Women (1971-74)*: The Committee suggested adoption of co-education at primary and secondary levels as a general policy, and recommended that common courses of general education be made available to both the sexes till class X.

— *National Commission on Self-Employed Women & Women in the Informal Sector (1987-88)*: The

Commission was of the opinion that education is an important instrument towards increasing and improving the chances of women's employability and for empowering them so that they become confident and further develop the capability to identify and contest areas of exploitation and discrimination. The Commission suggested steps to be taken for working women and their children, whereby they, and especially their girl children, may benefit. These include incentives for sending the girl-child to school such as midday meals, free textbooks and exercise-books, at least up to the primary level, syllabi suited to the students of rural areas, emphasis on the vocational aspects of education, scholarships for girls, and hostel facilities. The Commission's report was viewed by activists and the women's movement as 'fairly representative of the voice of women's movement, especially as it brought out the articulation of poor women in rural and urban areas sharply into focus'.

— *National Policy on Education (1986) & Programme of Action (1992)*: The National Policy on Education (1986) identified education as the agent of basic change in the status of women. Education was to be redesigned as a whole so that is could play an interventionist role in women's empowerment. Emphasis was laid on the participation of women in vocational, technical and professional education at different levels. Women were to be so educated that they had a positive self-image and were confident of themselves. At the societal level, group action was to be encouraged to ensure equal participation of men and women. Commenting on the Policy, one analyst argues that the incorporation of a section on Education for Equality in the New Education Policy of 1986 was a token gesture, included perhaps to partially offset the loss of political face by the Government of India's surrender to fundamentalist forces—with the enactment of the Muslim Women's (Protection of Rights on Divorce) Act in the same month. On the heels of the National Policy on Education of 1986 came the Programme of Action (1992), which emphasised education for women's equality, with priority to participation and empowerment.

— *National Commission for Women (1992)*: The National Commission for Women, established in January, 1992, set-up a Legal Unit to give shape to its objectives. It established institutional linkages with those concerned with women's issues, initiated studies on the impact of economic reforms on women, and focused on the gender perspective for the electronic and the print media.

The Commission has also sought to raise awareness regarding women's issues, apart from holding public hearings to ascertain the grievances of women. Yet, as "a subordinate agency of the Department of Women and Child Development", the National Commission for Women was "left... at the mercy of the bureaucracy". Ground realities while literacy rates have been on the rise since the turn of the century, for both males and females, census data show that the female literacy rate continues to lag behind.

The social attitude towards the girl-child is determined by factors of supply and demand. The demand factors include poverty situations, the family's inability to bear schooling costs for its children, poor health and lower status of women and anticipation of their discrimination in the job market. Supply side factors affecting the social attitude towards women's education include insufficient schools, distant location of schools (which makes parents apprehensive of sending young girls far away from home), inflexible school timings, and gender insensitive curricula.

A deficiency of female teachers is also thought to be a factor at work. However, there has been some improvement in this regard. While in 1986-87, 38 per cent of the primary school teachers were women. This improved to more than 50 per cent in 1997. Due to the play of varied factors, the drop out rate is higher for girls as compared to boys at every stage of school education. Almost three fourths of the girls drop out at the high school level.

WOMEN IN DAIRYING

The employment of women is an index of their economic and social status in society. In India, women constitute 90 per cent of marginal workers, with some regional variations. The Operation Flood (OF) programme recognises that:

— Dairying at the household level is largely the domain of women

— The products and income from dairying can be controlled by women

— Dairying can be practiced on a small scale. The prevailing dairy scenario presents many dilemmas.

— The first one is that modern dairying is geared to maximum production as opposed to traditional subsistence dairying.

— The second is that an expanding national herd of milch and other animals is dependent on diminishing and degrading common property resources for grazing and crop residues and other biomass.

- — The third is traditional dairying is largely dominated by men. All these have to be resolved within the framework of sustainable development.
- — The membership in most of India's 70,000 village-level dairy cooperative societies (DCS) is heavily dominated by men. The picture is now gradually changing in the favour of women. Efforts are on to give them their due place in dairy development. Presently, some 2,476 all-women DCS are functioning in the country in selected States. Out of 9.2 million total membership in DCS, 1.63 million are women (18 per cent). However, women constitute less than three per cent of total board members.
- — The poor rural households need a whole package of supporting inputs and services to develop dairying as an effective instrument of household livelihood. However, as the experience goes, these inputs are not always easily accessible to poor, rural women. Major factors that hamper the success of women's cooperatives are:
- — Resistance to women as cooperative members; women are yet to be recognised as farmers in their own right. In a mixed cooperative, lack of ownership of land prevents women not only from becoming member but also from obtaining credit, training, technical assistance. Women also do not have any say in the decision making policies of the cooperatives and thus cannot help formulate more policies to help themselves. Concrete strategies have to be devised to help women get ownership and control over productive assets, individually and collectively. It will be the single most important factor towards their empowerment and economic well-being. Some of these assets include a

plot of land, housing, workshed, animals and shareholding of cooperatives.

— Low literacy.

— Resistance from the upper socio-economic section of village community towards the poor.

— Access to finance (lack of): Small-farm household women need timely finance (credit) for short-term investments to manage their dairy enterprises in an efficient manner. For example, they cannot meet the needs of cattle feed, fodder and other essential inputs without ready cash. Facilities should also be made available for timely breeding of dairy animals and health care. A World Bank study of the OF project benefits in villages of Madhya Pradesh suggests that the lack of credit for the initial purchase of dairy animals remains a major constraint to OF's ability to reach the poorest households.

— Access to training facilities (lack of): Women should be imparted training in dairy husbandry, cooperative management and marketing. There is also a need for social organisation at the pre-cooperative stage to help in the formation of cooperatives as well as dissemination of the economics of dairy activity.

Role of SEWA

NGOs have played a leading role in cooperativising the women milk producers. They also assist in making the benefits of Government schemes available to poor milk producers. To name a few: The Andhra Pradesh Dairy Women's Programme, the Bhagavathula Charitable Trust's Women's Dairy Programme and SEWA's Women's Dairy Cooperatives.

National Dairy Development Board (NDDB) has initiated a special training programme for women . More than 860,000 women have participated in this educational programme. Still, most women producers do not always have access to training in modern livestock management.

SEWA is an organisation of 158,000 women workers in Gujarat in western India. Its experience in the arid zone of Banaskantha district has shown that among the many inputs, fodder is the key to milk production. This could also become part of the larger programme of ecological restoration. All the defunct primary societies in Radhanpur and Santhalpur talukas of the district were revived, strengthened and consolidated.

A fodder security system

To make dairying a significant source of income, it is realised that a Fodder Security System would have to be developed. This would provide nutrition to milch cattle, increase their milk yield and thereby the producers' income and stabilise the migrating households to receive benefits from the socio-economic infrastructure.

SEWA's fodder security system involves eight societies (five women's coops) who purchase fodder from fodder-surplus areas during the season, store it in a godown and distribute it on cash-and-carry basis, all the year round on no-profit, no-loss basis. This scheme is implemented by women members of SEWA now organised into DWACRA (Development of Women and Children in Rural Areas) Association.

The second stage of the Fodder Security System has been the plantation and cultivation of fodder. The DWACRA Association has got possession of the (defunct) four fodder farms (350 hectares of land) from the State Rural Development Corporation. The cultivation of fodder was started here in right earnest. Two other fodder farms, ten hectares each, are being maintained under the Government's Community Fodder Scheme by two of the Women's Dairy Cooperatives. This scheme has provided for 30 per cent of their fodder need during the first year itself.

Earlier, SEWA used to provide the revolving fund for the purpose. Now, 35 per cent of the investment is being done by women themselves. In some talukas, SEWA is also harvesting and helping drinking water supply. Additional employment is generated through home-based craft with assured marketing. The integrated approach of organising the rural women into their own economic bodies like Dairy Cooperatives, Savings and Credit Groups, labour unions and DWACRA Association has stabilised the families in their own homeland (migration has declined by about 80 per cent), regenerating their local ecology, and added income and assets worth Rs 30 million.

The erosion of traditional institutions for managing common property resources and the failure of new institutions to fill in the vacuum have affected adversely the natural resource base. The future of dairy industry lies in regenerating local ecology with the fullest participation of women and women's organisations

RURAL WOMEN AND BASIC FINANCIAL SERVICES

More than a billion poor people lack access to the basic financial services which are essential for them to manage their precarious lives. Good management of even the smallest assets can be crucial to very poor people, who live in precarious conditions, threatened by lack of income, shelter and food. To overcome poverty, they need to be able to borrow, save and invest, and to protect their families against risk. But with little income or collateral, poor people are seldom able to obtain loans from banks and other formal financial institutions. And even when they do have income or collateral, the amounts they require are often too small to appeal to banks.

Microfinance is one way of fighting poverty in rural areas, where most of the world's poorest people live. It puts credit, savings, insurance and other basic financial services within the reach of poor people. Through microfinance institutions such as credit unions and some non-governmental organisations, poor people can obtain small loans, receive remittances from relatives working abroad and safeguard their savings. Accessing small amounts of credit at reasonable interest rates gives people with the willingness and know-how an opportunity to set up a small business. Records show that poor people are a good risk, with higher repayment rates than conventional borrowers.

Need Credit to Rural Women

Rural women play a fundamental role in daily management of agricultural activities and of the family unit. They are however often confronted with numerous obstacles when applying for credit. Consequently, they try to optimise their possibilities of accessing credit from the various existing rural finance services:

- — The "unofficial" system (an alternative established by community members)
- — The "official" system (banks and other official financial institutions), and
- — Farmers' organisations which give loans to their members.

Rural women fulfil multiple functions on a daily basis: they are mothers providing for their family's well-being, farmers producing food for the family, shopkeepers supplying indispensable additional income. They are also in charge of natural resources management which ensures future food security for their families.

Although rural women represent a fundamental pillar for survival and management of the family unit, they are confronted with real difficulties in accessing additional resources such as credit. Various barriers arise when they try to undertake or develop any income-generating production activities.

Loans Facilitates to Rural Women

Loans play an important role in the economic, social and political improvement of the situation of women throughout the world. Improving rural women's access to finance gives them a chance to become autonomous. This can contribute to increase agricultural productivity, development of income-generating activities alongside their production activities, better control of production methods, and improved natural resource management. As a result they will be able to ensure food security for the future of which they are the guarantors.

Additional sources of finance can help in developing necessary commercial agriculture within the national and international context, whilst retaining subsistence farming for the community's daily needs.By increasing their economic power, they will be able to organise themselves more efficiently, to affirm their position as rural women farmers, to participate in decision-making processes and to draw up policies which concern them; as well as defending their own interests with public authorities and other relevant institutions.

Savings Facilitates for Rural Women

Savings are seen as insurance against foreseeable future

difficulties (constituting a dowry, bridging a difficult period, etc.) or completely unpredictable (food shortages, natural weather phenomenon, foodstuffs sold cheaply because of the death or accident of a member of the family, etc.). Rural women therefore insure themselves against future risks by saving in the form of land, herds, trees, gold jewellery, or by hoarding money, which also include risks such as theft, the compulsory gift of a sum to a member of the family in difficulty, a livestock epidemic, etc.

Access to safe and secure savings is an important part of addressing short-term, medium-term and long-term unforeseen circumstances. These savings allow them to protect their own funds and, as a result, to undertake other income-generating activities. Allowing them to control their incomes and to be paid for these activities, is to participate in granting autonomy to rural women.

Women's Responsibility in Agricultural Activities

Food crops are the basis of most rural production as they provide the necessary daily food rations for rural families. Within this context, women have a fundamental role in farming production activities, in particular looking after crops, and ensuring good management of these activities.

Faced with depletion of natural resources, men are increasingly forced to migrate and/or carry out non-agricultural activities in order to secure their livelihood. Rural women are therefore left to take on full responsibility for agricultural activities.

Savings/loan systems can therefore have considerable impact in such cases. For example, loans can enable the acquisition of a new technology or make it possible to hire labourers, thus allowing rural women to save time — hence reducing the fatigue of manual labour — in their agricultural activities. They can therefore retain their income-generating activities which they might otherwise have had to sacrifice in order to provide food.

Over and above their own economic interests, savings/loan facilities for rural women include much wider notions of political and social development such as time saving, family well-being and food security, improved finance management, personal autonomy and increased representation.

Sources of Finance

Women have several possible sources of finance at their disposal, each with its own advantages and disadvantages. The unofficial sector has always played an important part in financing rural women's activities. The different players in this sector are families, relatives or friends, private lenders including loan sharks, rural shopkeepers, and rural solidarity arrangements. The loans are thus either in money or in kind (for example loans of inputs reimbursed by harvested agricultural produce).

A new system of "semi-unofficial" micro-financing has also appeared during the last decade: the system set up by the non-government organisations which provide savings/loans to local rural and/or urban populations allowing populations who do not have access to the official sector to obtain loans at rates which are much better than in unofficial systems. We are including this finance model within the unofficial system as it was inspired from this system to better respond to the needs of the population. It attempts to correct the negative aspects whilst retaining the main operational methods.

The official sector includes country's various official banks (national banks, rural banks, etc.). Farmers' Credit Institutions exist alongside the systems mentioned above. They are specific to farmers' organisations and take the form of agricultural loans/savings institutions and cooperatives.

Whenever possible rural women use several savings/ loans strategies simultaneously, depending on their requirements, the amounts they may consider necessary, their reimbursement capabilities according to redemption dates, and as a function of their assessment of the risks they are taking in borrowing from the different finance systems.

At present, National economies are in the process of addressing the phenomenon of internationalisation and its implications for the rural economy. Savings/loan systems can play an important role in avoiding the marginalisation of rural women by their partial or total lack of integration into economic and marketing streams at the local, provincial and national level.

Savings/Loans in the Unofficial Finance Sector

Small farmers have always set up unofficial micro-finance systems, even before experts in the field of development made this one of its favorite themes. To begin with, these were only bartering systems, before the unofficial finance system developed into proper loans which could be large sums of money.

Despite the constraints of this system, the unofficial sector is still today widely used and very useful for small producers and for rural women in particular. Moreover, since there are numerous obstacles preventing access to the official credit system, many people retain the unofficial system as a source of savings and loans even if this alternative has a number of negative implications.

Rural Women and Unofficial Finance System

Rural women often use this system as they need small

amounts of cash and the loans are granted according to social, relational and cultural conditions, and not according to purely economical conditions which would not allow women to benefit from them.

They also constitute personal savings funds which enable them to address their family's basic needs. These savings, if they are not hoarded or invested in material goods (herds, gold, or land etc), can be invested in the unofficial sector (private loans, relatives; tontines) and are generally given in the form of loans to another person.

Thus the unofficial sector functions as real banks with their own savings and loan criteria depending on the socio-economic context of the region in which it develops, and it is successful because it is appropriate to the local situation.

Revolving loans and savings associations meet both economic and social needs are very common in developing countries. There have considerable impact for rural women who have their own funds and control the use of them. Through women's groups they are also empowered to manage, to be represented and to make claims and demands and are thereby no longer alone to face obstacles encountered in their daily lives.

This revolving system of savings/loans is a basic element in the life of rural women and allows numerous activities to emerge from these funds which can sometimes attain quite high levels.

The following are the various obstacles to the unofficial finance system's efficiency:

— Numerous studies, mainly carried out by universities and non-government organisations, have highlighted obstacles in the unofficial savings/loans systems. According to purely economic criteria, the impact of loans is limited, partly because unofficial systems imply limited capital and high costs which do not permit the development of large-scale activities.

— Moreover the system usually lacks reliability through insecurity of deposits and the lender's more or less good management of his finance system.

— Although the loans are granted at high interest rates, there is virtually no remuneration for savings.

— Apart from the development of community relationships, one of the possible negative points that can be noted is the social dependence which comes about due to the existing relationships with the person who has facilitated and/or made the loan.

— Finally, by using the unofficial finance system, rural women are not integrated into the official finance system and their economic activities continue to be marginal. Therefore, their activities remain on a small scale and cannot develop in a satisfactory manner.

The unofficial finance system is interesting in that it constitutes a recourse in the event of sudden difficulties. Its impact remains limited also because of the essential role of the personal relationships played in granting loans.

Role of Official Financial Systems

The official system (public or private national banks, rural banks, or development banks) can ensure more ambitious financial services than unofficial systems. However, using them may be difficult for rural women.

As rural women are increasingly in charge of the family farm's general management (rural exodus of men) and have to deal with the official finance system, facilitating access to loans could be a driving force in developing their production and processing activities, and in progressing towards agriculture for the local market.

Obstacles in the official finance system

Rural women have little access to information concerning official savings/loans institutions. In fact banks have a considerable communication problem with the rural environment in general, and with women in particular. The rare extension programmes concern their operating and financial services, targeting mainly farmers, without worrying about the specific nature of female problems. This means that rural women have a very limited idea of the nature of institutional savings/loans facilities.

Rural women are often considered as being insolvent because they are subsistence farmers, and are seen as a high-risk population for finance institutions.

Banks and financial institutions hesitate to grant loans to women, as they are usually small loans and do not provide a good enough return for the banks.

They are heavy institutional constraints such as administrative procedures and the necessity for guarantees (land ownership title deeds). With the problems of illiteracy and the lack of management knowledge, rural women are discouraged from accessing these financial services. Of course groups of women have a better chance of being provided with credit, but this necessitates organising women inside the community and this is not yet common practice.

Perhaps the most difficult of obstacles to be cleared are those of a socio-cultural nature. It is particularly complex for rural women to address the social practices of their communities and is a long-term challenge. These include standards and social rules (including land rights and inheritance procedures), religious practices and cast systems, social taboos, prejudice against women and rural women in particular.

Lastly is the classical difficulty of all rural populations, and not necessarily specific to rural women. Banks rarely have agencies in rural zones and women therefore have to go to towns which often mean walking for many hours. This is the case not only to open an account or ask for a loan, but also whenever they make a deposit, require information, or have a request. To add to the cost in time and in transport, one must also add the social cost as many prejudices exist concerning rural women going to the town and the economic cost of their absence from their families with regard to their daily domestic tasks and production.

Difficulties in accessing loans encountered by rural women reduce the scope of their initiatives, block their economic and social development, with the result that they are kept in a state of dependency and daily insecurity.

Agricultural Organisations are Finance services

Specialised in the rural sector's problems, agricultural organisations are characterised by the fact that they are set up, owned, managed and controlled by their members. As they are independent and democratically operated, they can set up credit policies and programmes which are better adapted to rural environments and to rural women when their voices are heard. They are consequently an extremely important element for implementing rural policies and defending the interests of all farmers, women and men. Agricultural organisations have multiple sectors of intervention and can set up genuine rural development programmes. Loans are one of the tools used in a general rural development policy, working towards solving the various economic, political, technical, social and cultural difficulties of this sector. However, setting up such a programme of associating savings/loans for the development of other income-generating activities or parallel activities (training, techniques, nutrition, health etc) requires several conditions for success.

Rural women's representation in agricultural organisations

To ensure a better participation, it is important that borrowers—and women in particular—take part in the assessment of savings/loans programmes so that they are involved in their sound management and therefore of their sustainability. Moreover, as there is no typical finance model, this active participation enables actual local needs to be identified and the best-adapted savings/loans system to be provided.

This is particularly true when the target population are rural women whose specific needs are not yet clearly defined. As the members of these organisations are in control of the policies set up, it is absolutely essential that agricultural organisations facilitate greater representation of rural women as members, allowing them to be represented in decision-making processes and on management committees.

Equal opportunities for men and women in becoming members of and participating in farmers' organisations are a fundamental precondition for success. Rural women need to be active within decision-making structures to be able to draw up savings/loans policies which really meet their specific needs.

A rural development programme including financial services should associate these services with improved access to inputs, land, technologies and training. It is very important for rural women to have full and direct access to the different services as members in their own right and not as wives of member farmers. This would enable them to have real control over the use of these facilities, in particular with respect to finance granted to them.

Taking the family unit into account

In rural development programmes, efforts should be made to develop savings/loans facilities for the whole family unit, with lines of credit specifically for women. This will mean less divisions within the family, the community and society as a whole.

Also, implementing a rural finance programme for women should entail considerations on maintaining the right balance between food production and commercial production so as not to affect family food and nutritional security. Such programmes should allow all daily activities of the rural woman to be linked together without endangering family unit's working and living conditions.

Training of and information for rural women

As regards training, extension and information on credit facilities from agricultural organisations, these should be adapted to the differences in men and women's knowledge, to their different activities and to their daily planning.

Agricultural organisations must therefore take into consideration the issues of rural women when drawing up policies which are more in keeping with their needs and requirements and thereby reducing the existing inequalities between men and women's access to their various facilities.

Under these conditions, finance can have a considerable direct impact on the life of farming families and on women in particular.

7

Women's Political Participation

The development context of women's political participation at the community and national levels will be reviewed for nuanced understanding of the nature of women's participation and their share in development processes and outcomes. With an increasing recognition among international community of women's historic exclusion from structures of power, a global commitment has been made to redress gender imbalance in politics. Women's enhanced participation in governance structures is viewed as the key to redress gender inequalities in societies.

Women constitute half of the world population and therefore, it is only fair that they should have equal participation and representation in world democracies. Instrumentalist argument pushed for women's greater participation on the essentialist ground that men and women are different. Women have different vision and concepts of politics owning to their sex and their gender roles as mothers. Therefore, it is assumed that women in politics will bring a special caring focus and female values to politics.

The roots of women's participation in politics can be traced back to the nineteenth century reform movement.

This movement emerged as a result of conflict between the Indian bourgeoisies, trying to wrest control from the British. This class made attempts to reform itself, mainly by campaigning against caste, polytheism, idolatry, animism, purdha, child marriage, sati etc., perceived as elements of primitive identity. Raja Ram Mohun Roy focused on two issues, namely women's education and abolition of sati.

In the early 1850s, a campaign on widow remarriage was launched resulting in the passage of a Bill in 1856, which allowed widow remarriage. This Bill though helped the situation of widows, denied them the right to their husbands' or his family's properties. Several eminent women reformers participated in this movement as well as in the religious reform movement of this period. Pandit Ramabai, Manorama Majumdar, Sarala Debi Goshal who started Bharata Stree Mahamandal for the education of women, Swarna Kumari Debi who started the women's organisation Sakhi Samiti in 1886 for widows are few examples. These activities gave momentum to women's participation in public spaces, which paved the way for their entry into the independence struggle. Swarna Kumari Debi, one of the two delegates elected from Bengal to represent the State at the 1890 Congress session is a case in point.

WOMEN IN THE INDEPENDENCE MOVEMENT

The *Swadeshi* movement in Bengal (1905-08) marked the beginning of women's participation in nationalist activities. Many of the women were from families involved in nationalist politics. Middle class nationalist women contributed jewellery, money and even grain to the movement. They took active part in the boycott of foreign goods and in revolutionary activities. Sister Nivedita is reported to have become a member of the

National Revolutionary Council and in that capacity, organised women for nationalist activities.

Like her there were several others seen as a threat by the British including Agyavati in Delhi, Madame Cama who was described by the Government as the recognised leader of the revolutionary movement and Kumudini Mitra who started a journal called *'Suprabath'* which linked nationalist politics to women's traditional power. Madame Cama, a Parsi woman nationalist persuaded the International Socialist Congress to support the Indian Independence Movement and also began a monthly journal called *'Vande Mataram'* towards this end.

The movement for independence also gave rise to the question of women's suffrage. In December 1917, Annie Besant and few other women met Mr. Montague to demand voting rights for Indian women. During the same period several all-India women's organisations came into being. In 1917, Annie Besant, Dorothy Jinarajadasa, Malathi Patvardhan, Ammu Swaminathan, Mrs. Dadabhoy and Mrs. Ambujamal founded the Women's Indian Association. Described as the first truly feminist organisation in India, it strongly supported the Home Rule Movement. In 1926, the All India Women's Conference was formed and became extremely active on the question of women's suffrage, labour issues, relief and nationalist work.

The 1920's also witnessed a second generation of feminists who were advocates of women's rights. Rajkumari Amrit Kaur, Lady Piroj Bai Mehta, Mrs. N. Sengupta, were some of the prominent women activists of this period. Several other women were active on causes other than the Independence movement including Prabhavati Mirza, Kamini Roy, and Aghorekamini Roy. A number of these reformist and revolutionary women were also eminent writers. Nagendrakala Mustafi,

Mankumari Basu, Kamini Roy, Kasibhai Kanitkar, Mary Bhore, Godavaribai Samaskar, Kamala Sathianandan, Rameshwari Nehru, Roopkumari Nehru, Parvatibai and Rukmanibai are examples of this stream of women activists who combined activism and writing.

Women who were strong leaders in the Independence movement were Sarojini Naidu, Kamaladevi Chattopadhyay, Aruna Asaf Ali, and Basanti Devi. A strong supporter of women's rights, Sarojini Naidu worked with the Congress and the Muslim League. She was instrumental in the passage of a resolution to support women's franchise and became the first Indian woman to become the elected President of the Indian National Congress. Kamaladevi Chattopadhyay participated in the *Satyagraha* movement of the 1930s. Aruna Asaf Ali's first major political involvement was in the salt march at which she was arrested and prosecuted. She was also active in the Quit India movement, edited *Inquilab* magazine of the Congress and established the National Federation of Indian Women. She came to be known as the Grand Old Lady of the Independence Movement and heroine of the 1942 movement. Basanti Devi took active part in anti-British activities and was arrested for picketing foreign goods shops, and in 1922 presided over the Bengal Provincial Congress Committee.

Thousands of women joined in the salt *Satyagraha*, which is "generally remembered as the first time 'masses of Indian women' got involved in the struggle for Independence". Several women's organisations were formed to mobilise women to participate in nationalist activities including processions, pickets, and *charka* spinning such as the Ladies Picketing Board, Desh Sevika Sangh, Nari Satyagraha Samiti and Mahila Rashtriya Sangh. Beyond any doubt, the active participation of women in the political struggles for independence consummated in a Constitution based on the principles of equality and guaranteeing equal rights to suffrage for women, in the year 1947 itself.

WOMEN'S PARTICIPATION IN POST-INDEPENDENCE

Though the foundation for political participation of women was laid down during the nationalist movement, there was no follow up or concerted effort to broaden the political base by incorporating women into political processes after independence. The space for women in the political arena has declined since independence and their participation in politics has been limited to family connections rather than convictions and commitment.

Women have been promoted to political positions only when there were no other male member available to continue the family's distinctive place and thus, as a devise to perpetuate the privilege of the family. By putting women in these positions, the family could still have control over the powers rested with the office. The framers of the Constitution perhaps believed that law would lead to social change and bring about equality between the sexes.

Yet inequality and discrimination continues to persist in all spheres of public and private life. This is quite evident from the fact that the participation of women in politics and in other decision-making bodies after attaining independence is very limited. Given this situation, the State has to take some corrective actions to ensure that women participate equally in the political sphere. Also, it is imperative to adopt certain affirmative action to eliminate the existing discrimination to ensure political equality as guaranteed in the Constitution.

The government of India, noting the low participation of women in politics; acknowledging the recommendations of the Committee for Status of Women Report, 1974; and drawing from the pioneering experience of

Karnataka which provided reservation for women in its three tier Panchayat Raj system (institutions of local selfgovernance) in the year 1983; adopted an affirmative action for providing reservation for women in these institutions in the year 1993.

The 73rd Constitutional Amendment Act introduced not less than 33 per cent reservation for women in the Panchayat Raj institutions in the rural areas. Similarly, the 74th Constitutional Amendment Act introduced similar reservation for women in Nagar Palika and Municipalities in towns and urban areas. With these Constitutional Amendments, over three million women are now actively participating in shaping the policies and programmes of the country, though only at the local levels of governance. However, such affirmative action is lacking at the higher echelons of governance at the State and Central levels.

Prior to the 73rd and 74th Constitutional Amendments, only the State of Karnataka had reservation for women in institutions of local self-governance. The Janata Party Government in Karnataka in 1991 passed a Bill to implement 25 per cent reservation for women in local elections. This spurred a national debate on the issue of reservation for women in several other states. For example, Sharad Pawar (Congress-I) announced 30 per cent of seats in Municipal Corporations and the Panchayat Raj Institutions to be reserved for women in Maharashtra. Following these initiatives, the 73rd and 74th Amendments were passed. It became mandatory that elections to these bodies be held once every five years. However, many states have sought to and even succeeded in circumventing this provision.

Assam, Arunachal Pradesh and Pondicherry have not held panchayat elections since the 73rd amendment came into force. In the case of Assam, where elections were due in 1997, they have been postponed first due to the budget session, then owing to the monsoons and, finally, because of the law and order situation in the state. Until recently, even Andhra Pradesh and Bihar belonged to the same category and held elections only after the intervention of the High Court and Supreme Court respectively. Further, states implementing the Panchayati Raj/Nagarpalika Acts show variation in their numbers as well as in their participation.

QUOTAS FOR WOMEN

The issue of separate political reservation for women came up during the course of the nationalist movement in the 1920s. The principal reason for opposing the idea of reserved seats was that it deflected from the demand for universal adult franchise and to stand for elections on the same terms as men. Besides, it was felt that there should be no hint of succumbing to the British strategy of "divide and rule" by referring to divisions within the national movement. "The public, official language of politics especially before a colonial government, had to be a language of equality and for fundamental rights of citizenship irrespective of sex, caste, religion or creed."This opinion was supported by the prominent and leading women's organisations of the time (All India Women's Conference, the Women's Indian Association and National Council of Women in India) and by the Home Rule League, the Indian National Congress and the Muslim League.

In 1932, a Joint Memorandum on the Status of Indian Women from the all-India women's organisations to the Franchise Committee set up at the end of the Second Round Table Conference expressed their demand for universal adult franchise "irrespective of any property or literacy qualification, with no expedients such as nomination or reservation of seats". The women's organisations also endorsed the declaration of the Fundamental Rights to Citizenship in India made by the Karachi session of the Indian National Congress, 1931, which called for equality before the law, irrespective of religion, caste, creed or sex, universal adult franchise and women's right to vote, represent and hold public office.

However, in the face of opposition from the British, the women's organisations agreed to a compromise which restricted the right to vote for women in the urban areas. The assumption was the urban women would be in a better position to represent the women of India. But the opposition to reservation remained and merit was to be the only criterion. It is, however, important to note that the opposition to the idea of reservation was not restricted to the question of women alone.

The All-India Women's Conference (AIWC) in their resolution expressed their opposition to the British "Communal Award" of 1932 which sought to provide separate electorates and reserved seats to Anglo-Indians, Christians, Muslims and Sikhs, and for the "depressed classes". The rationale behind such opposition was that divisions along the lines of religion, caste and sect would weaken the struggle against colonial rule and that legislatures must be filled by those who would rise above personal or communal considerations and think of the country's best interests. There were dissenting voices: Begum Sakina Mayuzada felt that desiring the good of one's community need not be at the cost of inflicting harm on others; and K.B. Firozuddin felt that the comparative educational backwardness of Muslim women might put them at a disadvantage in joint electorates. A separate resolution calling for the abolition of untouchability was adopted.

Women's organisations like the AIWC shared these perceptions. It is important to note, however, that the nationalist movement did arrive at a consensus on the issue of affirmative action or reservation for the depressed classes and this was given a constitutional status in 1950, when special provisions for the "scheduled castes" and "scheduled tribes" were written into the Constitution of India. These groups were to be given reservation in the parliament, state legislatures, education and employment in proportion to their population. Thus, while Article 15(1) of the constitution prohibits discrimination on the grounds of religion, sex, caste, birth and a host of other factors, Article 15(4) states: "Nothing in this article ..... shall prevent the State from making any special provisions for the advancement of any socially and educationally backward classes of citizens or for the Scheduled Castes and Scheduled Tribes". Likewise, Article 15(3) lays down the basis for the state making special provisions for women and children.

The Committee on the Status of Women in India (CSWI) 1974

The question of women's reservations came up once again in the Committee on the Status of Women in India (CSWI) in 1974. The Report noted that in spite of equal rights and universal adult suffrage guaranteed by the Indian constitution, women's presence in the state and central legislatures had been declining steadily over 25 years. While the Committee recorded arguments in favour of reservations, mainly by women activists, women legislators were of the opinion that women's reservation would be retrogressive and would contradict the principle of equality guaranteed in the constitution. Those who are against any form of affirmative action, particularly in public or government service, often take recourse to Article 15(1) or Article 16.

The dominant opinion in the CSWI was against reservations, though there were two notes of dissent. The arguments in favour of reservations dealt with: (a) the difficulties of women to gain entry into male-dominated political parties and hence the necessity of reservations; (b) that reservations for women would ensure a significant presence enabling women to act as an important pressure group; and (c) the presence of a critical mass of women would heighten the sense of responsibility among women and this would ensure that women's interests would be adequately represented.

The arguments against reservations were: (a) reservations for women would be a departure from the constitutional principle of equality; (b) women's interests cannot be isolated from the economic, social and political interests of groups, strata and classes in the society and linked to this was the notion that women are not a community, they are a category; and (c) systems of special representation for women may spiral into similar such demands from other groups and interests and thus threaten national integration.However, there was agreement on the need for reservations for women in the local bodies so as to ensure the interests of rural and poor women.

The two notes of dissent in the CSWI are very significant because they mark a shift in the perception of the "daughters of independence" generation and also because they raise questions about the way political representation has functioned. Sarkar and Mazumdar note with disarming and refreshing candour that as members of the pre-independence generation, they had never been supporters of special representation and that they had in academic discussions criticised the system of reservations for scheduled castes and scheduled tribes as "... a legacy of the colonial period which institutionalised the backwardness of certain sections of our population". However, the reality has forced them to take a fresh look at the question.

The main reasons for dissenting with the majority opinion within the CSWI also arise out of and are consistent with the findings of the Committee; that is, despite progressive legal changes, the actual situation of the mass of Indian women has not changed significantly and the continuing under-representation of women prevents them from participating in the decision-making process of the country.

Women in Local Self-Government

The recommendations of the CSWI remained in cold storage till the early 1990s, when the Indian Parliament passed the Seventy-Third Amendment to the Indian Constitution with near unanimity in December 1992 and the Amendment came into effect from 24 April 1993. The purpose of this amendment was to revitalise local self-governing village councils (which had been in existence in some states of the country even prior to this amendment). The Seventy-Third Amendment has been considered historic and one of the most significant attempts at transforming the Indian polity in the direction of greater democratisation and decentralisation of powers. It has also been regarded as an important instrument for drawing in the vast sections of marginalised people in the task of selfgovernment.

The amendment has mandated a wider representation for historically marginalised and excluded groups like the scheduled castes, the scheduled tribes and women thus deepening the roots of democracy. Following the amendment, people from the scheduled castes and tribes are now represented in proportion to their population in the area of the panchayat (village council)—in its membership and in proportion to their population in each state in the positions of the chairpersons of these panchayats; one-third seats are reserved for women in general in each panchayat, that is, at the village cluster level, at the block level, and at the district level. Women from the scheduled castes and the scheduled tribes have similar one-third reservation in the positions reserved for these communities. Finally, there is one-third reservation for women among the positions of the chairpersons of these bodies.

The reservation is to be rotated among the various constituencies and panchayats to ensure the widest spread. Regular elections are to be held every five years and financial resources are to be devolved by the setting up of state finance commissions and central finance commissions. The states have been mandated to make the panchayats institutions of self-government and to give them responsibility for planning and implementation of schemes for economic development and social justice for which appropriate functions and responsibilities have to be devolved. The constitutional amendment was soon followed by state-level legislation, which brought their panchayat laws in conformity with the requirements of the constitution. The logic behind the system of reservations is that institutionalised inequalities require institutionalised countermeasures from above to ensure some semblance of genuine democracy.

Women in Local Self-Governing Institutions

The most significant and new feature has been bringing about a certain uniformity regarding representation of the weaker sections. While reservation of seats for scheduled castes and tribes has been written into the constitution from the very outset, the reservation for women is new and the most important contribution of the amendment. According to many analysts, it has brought a critical mass of women to these institutions and holds forth tremendous potential. In 1994 and 1995, the first round of elections to the panchayats was held and nearly one million women entered the threshold of political institutions of local self-government. The second round of elections to the local bodies was concluded in 2000.

What has been the experience of women's participation for the first time in these institutions, both in terms of transforming these institutions and for the women themselves? This will have to be assessed in terms of India's traditional social structure, which is characterised by a socially legitimised hierarchy, based on the caste system, an integral element of which has been gender discrimination. The caste-based social order still holds its sway in India's society and politics, in spite of the fact that the Indian constitution is a democratic constitution which upholds equality of all and forbids discrimination on the basis of caste, class, creed or gender.

Women's marginalisation is almost a given in the Indian social situation. Given this, has the formal change brought about a significant change in this situation? Evaluations done on women's participation in the PRIs have highlighted the following dimensions.

1. Women have responded overwhelmingly and participated with full enthusiasm in the elections and in the proceedings of the PRIs, thus exploding the myth that women were uninterested in politics and public life. There is a near-unanimous opinion amongst the women that they would have been unable to get into these bodies were it not for statutory representation.
2. While there is a great degree of variation across the different states in the country, nonetheless one generalisation can be made—approximately about 40 per cent of the women who have got into these bodies come from marginalised sections and communities, though the positions of chairpersons

tended to be occupied by women from the more well-to-do sections of rural society, like well-off middle peasant families.

3. The women representatives generally got the support of the families during the elections and also in the performance of their new political roles. Marginalised sections like the scheduled castes and tribes saw the women from their groups as representatives of the interests of their group in the political arena, while the better-off sections saw the women from their own groups as helping to consolidate their positions.
4. The self-esteem of the women has gone up tremendously, and that is an observation that holds true across the board. The stepping of women into the public realm has long-term implications for gender relations in society and the family. There are already small but significant changes as men take over some roles within the family when women go to attend meetings.
5. While the presence of women in these institutions over the last eight to nine years has not transformed the power structure in the rural areas in any significant manner, and vested interests have tried to use the provision for women's reservation to consolidate their position, the overall experience has been positive. Thus women are engaging in power struggles that used to be dominated by men, sometimes as actors and at other times as pawns. However, participation in the public realm for women means that hitherto marginalised groups and communities are finding a legitimate space to articulate their interests and aspirations, and the women of these groups are getting politicised, although slowly.

But regarding the question of women's empowerment: (a) Are women beginning to break their silence, to challenge patriarchal ideology? (b) Are they beginning to transform institutions and structures of gender subordination and inequality? (c) Are the new women in panchayats beginning to gain access and control over material and knowledge resources and altering their self-image? (d) Are they gaining new skills and gaining self-confidence? (e) Are they succeeding in avoiding cooption and dilution of the empowerment process by pervasive patriarchal forces with new ways of exercising power and becoming a political force?

Women's Reservation Bill

The Eighty-Fourth Constitution Amendment Bill meant to provide one-third reservation of seats to women in state and central legislative bodies and the current discussions and controversies around it mirror the contradictions of Indian society and the contestations in access to power and resources between those who have been traditionally excluded and the socially and politically dominant sections of Indian society. The Women's Reservation Bill once again throws up questions of certain kinds of identity, specifically caste and religious identity, the intermeshing of gender identity with caste and religion and their articulation in the public realm, in the field of politics. What is significant is the sea change in the attitude to the question of women's reservation among leading women's organisations and activists in key periods in the 1930s, 1970s and the 1990s. The core questions to our mind relate to the hierarchy of Indian society and the manner in which this hierarchy operates in the field of politics and political representation. It also raises questions about the nature of representation.

The near unanimous support for the Bill among national level women's organisations is premised on a certain understanding of the patriarchal forms of oppression and exclusion that characterise Indian society and the undeniable reality of declining participation of women in political life, specifically in the legislatures. And historically the suppression and exclusion of women has been extremely important in maintaining a Brahmanical and caste-dominated social order, and affirmative action for women will undoubtedly contribute towards the democratisation of society. The protagonists of the Bill highlight the traditionally sanctioned exclusion of women from the public sphere as crucial. However, emphasising the dimension of gender oppression at the expense of other oppressions (of caste, ethnicity, class, religion etc.) glosses over the complex and intricate ways in which gender oppression is embedded in these categories.

Historically, women's suppression has no doubt been very important in maintaining upper-caste exclusivity and hegemony. Affirmative action for women would certainly play a role in undermining male and upper-caste dominance. Even so, certain recent developments suggest the need for addressing gender oppression in more subtle and nuanced ways, if access to power and resources to all categories of women is to be ensured.

The continued dominance of the upper castes in education, administration and structures of government is a reality that cannot be glossed over. This has been paralleled by an increasing presence and visibility of women from the upper-caste middle classes. On the other hand, the women (and men) from the subaltern communities and classes have largely been victims of "development". Besides the neo-liberal paradigm combined with the ideology of a right wing, majoritarian, Hindutva nationalism has only exacerbated the caste, class, religious, ethnic, regional and gender divides with women being only more and not less embedded in their groups leading to much greater differentiation among women, which in turn has also meant a more diverse and varied political articulation.

The opponents of the bill in its present form point out that it is likely to exclude women from the "other backward classes" (OBCs) and the minorities. Almost all the political parties except the Communist Party of India (CPI) and the Communist Party of India (Marxist)—CPI(M)—are deeply divided on this issue. The Hindu nationalist party in government, the Bharatiya Janata Party (BJP) leadership, is in favour of the Bill in its present form, although one of its women members of parliament had expressed reservations to the Bill on the ground that OBC women were likely to get excluded. Needless to say, there is also a strong resistance on the part of a considerable number of political leaders to "encroachments" into what has been a traditionally male preserve.

The media has trivialised the debate by often characterising it as a battle between "feminists" and "casteists". The crux of the issue is whether indeed the generalised oppression and exclusion of women characteristic of society is a sufficient basis for transcending the divisions of caste, religion and ethnicity and whether indeed the women's movement is representative enough to effect such a unity. Unfortunately so far, the statements of leaders of women's organisations that support the Bill have not revealed enough awareness about the complexity of the problem nor even enough critical reflection about the variegated nature of gender relations among the OBCs and the minority communities.

The tendency on the part of women's organisations has been to point to stronger patriarchal norms prevalent among the OBCs and the Muslims and the attitudes of the men of these communities as being particularly "backward" and "male chauvinist", thus focusing on the family as the principal site of patriarchal control and oppression and ignoring its wider social context.The fact that the women and the men of these groups face the consequences of being at the lower rungs of a social hierarchy still principally dominated by upper castes and the reality and prospects of marginalisation as groups must surely affect the texture of gender relations.

Recent analyses of the Women's Reservation Bill raise important though disturbing issues regarding the relative ease with which the question of women's reservation has been accepted by the ruling elites in the 1990s, as compared to the resistance to this in the 1970s.Menon points to two developments which could explain the shift. First, the challenges to the authority and legitimacy of the nation state from various movements from below in the wake of continued economic and political crisis in the early to mid-1970s; the resurgence of backward caste movements, regional movements and radical left movements challenged the nation state and its legitimacy. Second, women emerged as a significant force in politics from the 1970s onwards. However, it is the changing composition of the parliament with a significant number of members from the backward castes, which challenges the hegemony of the upper castes and has made the question of women's reservation more acceptable.

Thus gender has been pitted against caste. And it is not a coincidence that this is accompanied by the rise to political dominance of right-wing Hindu chauvinist forces. Besides, there is another dimension: the fact that the women's movement is no longer perceived as a threat to the social order is also a result of the cooption of gender issues both by the state and the NGOs.

There are other opinions from women activists and scholars who seriously question the efficacy of reservations as an instrument for the achievement of the goal of equality. These scholars focus on the fact that even the experience with women's reservations in the institutions of local self-government has not been entirely positive and that women need to traverse a long road before they reach the portals of parliament. They point out to the loopholes in the manner in which Panchayat Raj institutions have functioned; the crying need for training of women and the need for greater gender sensitivity among the administration.

Besides, there is a feeling that if women want to be in national and state-level politics, they must fight their way up and as a first step they must fight for 33 per cent seats for women in the respective political parties. It is important to note that usually this reservation about quotas for women is also accompanied by a reservation about the whole question of quotas on the basis of caste. There is a fear that the question of women's reservations will raise the question of caste, religion and other divisive categories.

What is happening to Indian society is a criss-crossing of movements of various oppressed sections.Often these movements pull in different and even opposite directions, thus defeating the process of democratisation in the short run. It is a challenging task both for the leaders of these movements and social analysts to unravel the myriad oppressions that characterise Indian society and to draw out the major strand which will strengthen and contribute to the overall process of democratisation of society. The levers of change have to be sought in an overall democratisation of society. And this is even more so in a plural society like India where the political system has to ensure a modicum of equality between all groups if history's longest oppression is to be seriously tackled. This would imply that the struggle for gender equality and justice will have to be woven into the struggle for emancipation of each of the oppressed groups and communities.

WOMEN IN THE INDIAN LEGISLATURES

As in other parts of the world few women in India find a place in the lower house of parliament – the *Lok Sabha* in India. The *Lok Sabha* in 2002 had 8.8 per cent women placing India 82nd of the 180 countries for which data on women in the lower house is reported by the Inter-Parliamentary Union. For national elections in India too there is a gender gap as in countries like the US. Women have also turned out at lower rates than men for elections to the *Lok Sabha.* As Table 7.1 indicates, in all elections in Independent India consistently women have consistently turned out to vote less than men though the gap has become lower in the last two decades.

Table 7.1. Women's Representation in Parliament, 1952-2005

	Lok Sabha			*Rajya Sabha*		
Year	*Total Seats*	*Women Members*	*Per-centage*	*Total Seats*	*Women Members*	*Per-centage*
1952	499	22	4.4	219	16	7.3
1957	500	27	5.4	237	18	7.5
1962	503	34	6.8	238	18	7.6
1967	523	31	5.9	240	20	8.3
1971	521	22	4.2	243	17	7.0
1977	544	19	3.4	244	25	10.2
1980	544	28	7.9	244	24	9.8
1984	544	44	8.1	244	28	11.4
1989	517	27	5.3	245	24	9.7
1991	544	39	7.2	245	38	15.5
1996	543	39	7.2	223	20	9.0
1998	543	43	7.9	245	15	6.1
1999	545	49	9.0	245	19	7.8
2004	539	44	8.2	245	28	11.4
2005	545	45	8.2	245	28	11.4

Similarly, the presence of women in parliament has remained remarkably stable at 5 per cent until the 1990s when it averaged around 8 per cent. The smaller proportion of women who have a place in the *Lok Sabha* is replicated in the *Vidhan Sabhas* as well. Table 7.2 reports the number of women who are members of the legislative assemblies and it is clear that the proportion of women who find a place in these legislatures is low and remains in the single digits for almost every state. What is remarkable about this very low level of representation for women is that it occurs even in states like Kerala that have been hailed for their favourable treatment of gender concerns. While women indeed have achieved almost universal literacy in Kerala and are far more active in the labour force, their political presence in the legislative bodies is remarkably low.

Table 7.2. Women's Participation and Representation in State Assemblies

State	*Election Year*	*Turnout - Men*	*Turnout - Women*	*Percentage of Women in the State Legislature*
Andhra Pradesh	1999	72.07%	66.24%	9
Arunachal Pradesh	1999	72.38%	73.58%	3
Assam	2001	77.23%	71.82%	8
Delhi	1998	50.89%	46.41%	13
Bihar	2000	70.71%	53.28%	6
Goa	2002	69.90%	68.23%	3
Gujarat	1998	63.34%	55.03%	2
Haryana	2000	69.97%	67.85%	4
Himachal Pradesh	1998	70.26%	72.21%	9
Jammu & Kashmir	1996	60.57%	46.08%	2
Karnataka/Mysore	1999	70.62%	64.58%	3
Kerala	2001	74.39%	70.67%	6
Madhya Pradesh	1998	66.45%	53.53%	8
Maharashtra	1999	63.62%	58.03%	4
Manipur	2002	90.09%	91.07%	2
Meghalaya	1998	74.20%	74.83%	5
Mizoram	1998	76.42%	76.22%	0

Nagaland	1998	80.65%	77.07%	0
Orissa	2000	63.63%	54.25%	9
Punjab	2002	65.92%	64.27%	7
Pondicherry	2001	69.51%	70.70%	0
Rajasthan	1998	67.45%	58.88%	7
Sikkim	1999	84.36%	79.10%	3
Tamil Nadu	2001	61.30%	56.83%	11
Tripura	1998	81.96%	79.65%	3
Uttar Pradesh	2002	56.75%	50.33%	6
Uttaranchal	2002	55.96%	52.89%	6
West Bengal	2001	77.83%	72.53%	9

This difference, by itself, should give pause to arguments that seek to link women's education and employment to a place in public political life axiomatically. Table 7.2 provides evidence that Indian electoral politics is still the domain of men. Evidence from post election national surveys confirms this understanding. Table 7.3 reports the results of an analysis of a national post-election survey conducted in 1971. The table suggests that women were far less likely to say that elections influenced the government than men.

Table 7.3. Gender and the Influence of Elections on the Government

Issue	*Women answering Yes*	*Men Answering Yes*
Do you have a say in govt.	23	39
Do elections influence the govt.	32	53
Voting has an effect on govt. action	38	59

More than half of the men, in a post-election survey, said that elections could influence the government whereas less than a third of the women thought similarly. These differences held up when respondents were asked whether voting has any effect on government action. Finally, women also felt that they had less say in the government than men.

DECENTRALISATION OF DEVELOPMENT PLANNING

Decentralisation of development planning and implementation are central to both Panchayati Raj and the Guidelines. It is important therefore to examine the compatibility of the definitions of decentralisation, development and governance embodied in both systems. There are two main objectives of decentralisation: one is to enable communities to meet their basic needs to ensure physical well being and the other is the realisation of civil and political freedom, democracy and autonomy.

Whether these latter are included as an explicit purpose, and if so, whether they are included as fundamental rights or simply as laudable goals, affects the political character of the decentralisation programme. These questions address some fundamental issues: what counts as development? What role should the state play in development and what criteria should confine their areas of control?

The practical resolution of these issues in India has been especially influenced by two factors. The first, as partly explored in the last section, is pressure from state governments and sections of the electorate to devolve power. The second is pressure from international donors for the state to scale down direct implementation of development programmes. Donors have insisted that India decentralises management and works towards good governance, described as 'the manner in which power is exercised in the management of a country's economic and social resources'. The agenda for good governance includes a reformed public sector to ensure efficiency and transparency.

Development programmes should be implemented through cooperation between the state and institutions in civil society, especially NGOs. The logic behind the construction of these partnerships is that both the state and NGOs have comparative advantages which combined, can improve the delivery of development programmes. In particular, NGOs can ensure that projects stimulate 'participatory development' because they operate at a smaller scale, slower pace, and are more flexible and attuned to local needs.

State withdrawal in India is still slow, but the importance of involving NGOs was centrally accepted in the seventh five year plan and has been manifested in the rapid proliferation of NGOs during the late 1980s and 1990s. It is especially evident in programmes on poverty and the environment such as those for watershed management.

The governance agenda has a powerful influence on the way in which democracy and development are conceived in India. The governance agenda recognises the principle of democratic rights and the importance of accountability. However there is little consideration in the governance agenda of the role of democratic politics in deciding the principles of governance. 'The question of whether demands for governance—good, or efficient, or equitable—should emanate from the citizens of a polity, and exclusively from them, is not generally raised'.

The exclusion of politics results in a restrictive definition of democracy as defined by the formal institutions and procedures. PRIs are included in the system not as a check and balance on accountability, or as part of the procedure for making policy decisions, but as an implementing agency. There are several implications that can be drawn from this interpretation of democracy and development. The first is that development is not open to political contestation. The second is that good governance can ensure accountability and transparency. But to who? If institutions of governance are not accountable to the democratic polity (PRIs) then to who are they accountable? Third, and conversely, if the formal conditions of democracy are fulfilled, does 'good governance' necessarily follow? As Lateef observes, 'accountability exists in the formal sense in India. We have the option to "throw the rascals out" and frequently do. But accountability is eroded by the lack of true choice for voters'.

A democracy that ensures good governance, and accountability to voters, has to be politically contested and constituted. This conclusion was abundantly clear in the operation of the Panchayati Raj system in Karnataka The central question in most development projects today, which includes those for watershed management, is not how to work with the democratic system, but how to generate 'participation'. Participatory development describes the principle that people have to be part of the identification of their development needs and problems, and have to be part of the design for the solution.

The concept of participation has been much studied and different 'depths' of participation have been identified, ranging from 'passive participation' to 'self-mobilisation'. Participation is now identified, arguably, as the most important element in development programmes, and the lack of participation the reason that development programmes fail. There is no doubt that participation is important: but how do participation in democratic development and participation in development projects compare? An assumption of the participatory logic of the latter is implicit in the participatory logic of the latter is the assumption that the root cause of social problems can be located in local social attributes, rather than the structures, property regimes and social orientation of the state. Participation is intended to empower local people and enhance project effectiveness by ensuring that people have a stake in the project. Participation in this context is a component of a project and confined to implementation. The participatory process does not influence the definition of priorities at the district, state or national level, and as a component of an externally assisted programme, it is insulated from formal political processes.

The notion of what decentralisation entails, and how communities should participate, is a major difference between the Constitutional Amendment and the Guidelines. The usual reason given for not working through PRIs is that they are governed by elites and too corrupt. This logic assumes that governance can bring development, and that development should precede democracy. As Jayal notes a person becomes a 'citizen-in-the-making', 'a subject: a passive recipient of rights, enjoyer of governance, beneficiary of development'. Whilst this option sounds unattractive, there is plenty of evidence from East Asia that the benefits of state administered development can be substantial. There is also plenty of evidence from the early days of Panchayati Raj that the human costs of challenging power structures at the local level can be hard.

The difference is tangible. However in practice, both government officials and NGO interviewees saw the boundaries between the two as more fluid. They all agreed that democratic development is the final goal and that building local capacity could lead to this objective in a less confrontational, more efficient manner.

Decentralisation in practice

The 73rd Amendment provides for units of self-government that will fundamentally and permanently alter the democratic process. The 73rd Amendment has been widely welcomed as constituting landmark legislation which provides a constitutional basis and continuity to the Panchayati Raj system. It specifies that Panchayats shall be established throughout the country at all three tiers, that elections shall be held every 5 years, that one third of all elective seats shall be reserved for women and about 15-18 per cent for scheduled castes and tribes. It has specified a developmental role for Panchayats at all three tiers and a District Planning Committee to coordinate these. The 29 areas over which the PRIs have jurisdiction are provided for in the eleventh schedule of the constitution.

A state Election Commission has been established to supervise Panchayat elections and a state Finance Commission to make recommendations about the principles that should govern the distribution, sharing and raising of revenue. The state governments have been given considerable freedom over how the 'spirit' of the Amendments is to be implemented. These are specified in the Conformity Acts that the states are required to submit to the central government. As a long time observer of Panchayati Raj commented 'PRIs have now become an inalienable part of the Indian polity. We cannot work around them any longer. They are here to stay.'

These are all positive developments. Unfortunately there is a considerable gap between the spirit of the legislation and the manner in which it is being implemented. In almost all states the implementation of Panchayati Raj has gone through phases of focused attention and decline. Political parties often disable PRIs established by a previous government in order to disable what they perceive to be local power bases of that government. Political parties also frequently promise Panchayati Raj as part of their election manifestos, and then establish these in some form, however diluted, when they are elected. Both these swings are apparent in Karnataka and Andhra Pradesh.

Karnataka passed a very progressive Panchayati Raj Act in 1987 under the Janata Dal government that attracted attention all over the country because of its radical provisions for the devolution of power to districts and villages. The general approach was that any activity whose area of benefit did not extend beyond the district should be managed at that level. The DRDA was abolished and merged with the Zilla Parishad, which was given wide-ranging functions. Detailed orders were given by the state government specifying the programmes, personnel and funds of each department that would be put under the Zilla Parishad. The Adhyaskhsa was given the status of State Minister.

In Andhra Pradesh the Telugu Desam Party made a reconstruction of Panchayati Raj system part of their election manifesto in 1984. They created a third tier that brought 'government closer to the people' and held elections in 1986. There has been some progress in both states to implement the recommendations of the 73rd Amendments. However this is a slow process and many observers have commented that in both states PRIs are actually less decentralised, autonomous and progressive than before. In Karnataka the Congress government rolled back many of the provisions of the earlier act in the early 1990s. Some problems in the implementation of both the spirit and the latter of the law, which are common to most states. The broad areas of concern are:

— The lack of functional autonomy and poor identification of what constitutes self-government,

— The lack of financial autonomy,

— Lack of legal authority. Underlying all of these is political and bureaucratic opposition to the full-scale decentralisation of power.

Functional and administrative decentralisation

Although the Constitution identifies Panchayats as institutions of self-government, the scope of 'self-government' has not yet been defined. The state governments have been given the freedom to decide on the operation of PRIs and many have chosen to interpret self-government as 'agency for the implementation of development programmes'. The accepted norms of decentralised self-government are:

- — A function that can be done at a particular level should be done at that level and no higher,
- — The allocation of functions at the various levels should complement each other,
- — The line of command should be clear so that the autonomy of each tier is observed,
- — PRIs can never be units of self-government if they continue to function as agents of the government,
- — Local level planning of local resources should be an important function of Panchayats, and should be backed by financial and judicial powers.

In most states decentralisation has been limited to development works on the 29 subjects listed in the XIth Schedule, and even in this narrow domain the transfer of authority has been haphazard and the division of powers unclear. The state government retains the power to assign or withhold functions, which is constitutionally a job for the state legislatures. The bureaucracy has been reluctant to frame the rules for decentralisation and most poverty alleviation projects still flow through the DRDA. Watershed development, which is on the XIth Schedule, is a case in point.

Financial autonomy

Functional autonomy has little meaning unless it is

backed by financial autonomy. PRIs have survived mainly on 'grants-in-aid' from the central and state governments. Central funds for specific schemes are meant to flow directly to PRIs (through DRDAs if they exist) with Panchayats acting as the delivery agents for these schemes. In addition Gram Panchayats receive an annual grant from the state government. Under the 73rd Constitutional Amendment Gram Panchayats are eligible to raise revenue and to a share of state revenue. However the details of this are left to the state Finance Commissions and most of these have yet to specify their conclusions. Commentators have argued that the devolution of revenue-raising powers to the Gram Panchayats is critical.

Rajaraman et al. argue that fiscal devolution should be linked to the functions which are listed in the XIth Schedule. These subjects, such as levies on water resources, and royalties on the use of common property, constitute the 'natural domain' of local government. However presently they are being collected by the state. The approach paper to the ninth five year plan states that 'the Panchayati Raj Institutions must mobilise local resources and the State Act must empower them to levy taxes and cesses at different levels'.

Further that 'in the case of Centrally Sponsored Schemes, it is proposed that during the ninth plan the flow of funds would be directly tied to the Panchayati Raj Institutions'. Revenue collection from; water, forests and other common resources are not so complicated and have the potential to provide large revenue to the Gram Panchayats. The ability to raise revenue, or to collect public contributions, is important not only as a source of income but as a means through which to promote participation. It is also a means through which to promote accountability to local people.

Judicial autonomy

Finally, the transformation of PRIs into units of self-government is hindered by their lack of judicial autonomy. Local self-government without any policing or judicial powers lack credibility, and therefore one of the provisions that many observers have stressed is essential are Nyaya Panchayats; a system of decentralised justice.

Decentralisation and the guidelines

The Guidelines provide for a devolution of decision-making powers to the district and for the transfer of funds from the central government, along with the share from the state government, to the district, and from there directly to the Watershed Committees. As such it is no different from most of the poverty alleviation programmes which run through the DRDA. The Guidelines also specify that the Watershed Committee should open a bank account for the receipt of money for watershed development.

Another interest bearing account is to be opened for money generated by the project in contributions, user fees etc., to be used for post-project watershed maintenance. Both funds are under the management of the Watershed Secretary, a member of the Wasteland Development Team, and the chairman of the Watershed Committee. This provision for decentralisation of funds is new. So is the emphasis that the Guidelines place on co-operation between government institutions, NGOs, and PRIs.

The extent to which the Guidelines are able to ensure decentralised watershed development is limited by several factors. First, the Watershed Secretaries, PIAs, Watershed Development Trusts (WDTs), WAs, and WCs are all approved from the hierarchy above them. All of these institutions are dependent on the hierarchy for funds and are in the final instance accountable to the government. The tendency for the Collector to retain control over decision-making persists in the implementation of the Guidelines. 'Collectors continue to retain control over decision-making processes, rather than moving towards a more facilitative and supportive role emphasising a decentralisation of power and responsibility'. The extent to which the Guidelines can ensure watershed management can only be judged by what remains in terms of physical or institutional capacity and structures once the project withdraws.

The Guidelines specify throughout that the PR institutions can, may, and should be involved in the implementation of watershed development programmes. However without specifying their areas of authority the Guidelines leave the operation of the Guidelines to the status quo in power relations, and in most states the upper hand is held by the state administration.

— There are several areas in which immediate questions arise. The Guidelines provide for the establishment of a District Watershed Development Advisory Committee (DWDAC). The 73rd Constitutional Amendment provides for the establishment of a District Development Committee (DDC). The XIth Schedule lists watershed development as one of its areas of control. Is this a duplication of activities?

— The Guidelines state that 'the DRDA/ZP, as the case may be, shall be responsible for the implementation of these Guidelines at the district level.' The ZP can be responsible for the implementation of the watershed programme 'once they come into operation with adequate powers and resources'. Where the DRDA has been made responsible, the Chief Executive Officer will be a member of the advisory committee. 'The Zilla

Parishad at the district level and the Panchayat Samiti at the block level shall have the right to monitor and review the implementation of the programme'.

— WIs have the right to register themselves, and are encouraged to do so in the Guidelines. Sporadic efforts have also been made to federate these groups at the district and sub-district level. As independent organisations these groups can federate at whatever level they want to, but if they are supported by development organisations and donors then they may conflict with higher level PRIs. The PRIs have been created for decentralised development so perhaps there should be more of an explicit appreciation of their ability to provide the umbrella institution. The Karnataka Panchayati Raj Act through an Amendment in 1997 provides for committees to be set up by the GP for specific purposes with provisions to have non-elected persons to be members. This arrangement has been provided to fill the gap that existed at the village level of any institutional arrangements to involve the community in development work.

— The ninth plan provides for the provision of funds for centrally sponsored schemes to go directly to Panchayati Raj Institutions. Interviewees from the Department of Rural Development (DRD) in New Delhi confirmed that this was being considered. How will this be coordinated with the funds going for watershed development? What is the position of the state governments on this? All of the interviewees from state governments saw the devolution of funds to the district level (whether PRI or DRDA) as, in the words of one interviewee 'a vote of noconfidence against the state'. They considered it to have detrimental affects for the evolution of decentralised government.

Institutional Change, Cooperation and Conflict

The pressure for institutional change in development planning and implementation, has come both from international donors and from internal political and economic pressure. Within Indian State Governments, regional movements, and an increasingly mobilised electorate have put pressure on the central government to decentralise. International donors have at the same time placed pressure on the government to continue economic liberalisation and to scale down the public sector. The emphasis is no longer on state withdrawal but on public sector reform and capacity building.

This change in perspective is partly due to revisionist perspectives on the role of the state inspired by development in East Asia and the role of state bureaucracies in enabling this. Empirical and conceptual work arising from the new institutional economics framework has also challenged the dominant role ascribed to the market during the 1990s. The general trend has been to a reconsideration of the role of the state, rather than prescribing its withdrawal. 'Matching role to capability involves not only what the state does but also how it does it. Rethinking the state also means exploring alternative instruments, existing or new, that can enhance state effectiveness'.

These ideas provide the official context of development policy and the operating principle for donors. In India the importance given to institutional cooperation in development planning is manifested in the eighth and ninth five year plans and in the rapid growth of NGOs involved in poverty alleviation projects throughout the 1990s.

The rethinking of the role of the state has led to a large literature on cooperation between the state and civil society institutions. The role that political institutions should play in this collaboration is less evident. The importance of 'democracy' and of social movements is generally recognised but the practical role of politics or of local political institutions remains unexplored.

This policy failure to examine the role that political institutions should play in the development programmes is reflected in the discussion around the implementation of the Guidelines. The theoretical and practical concentration has so far been on the role that the government should play, where and how it should cooperate with the voluntary sector, and in which areas there is a need for capacity building. However, as White argues, an effective crafting of institutions requires us 'to think systematically about the political dynamics of democracies in developing societies'.

TRANSFORMING WOMEN

Women's experience of PRI has transformed many of them. The elements of this transformation include empowerment, self-confidence, political awareness and affirmation of identity. Women have gained a sense of empowerment by asserting control over resources, officials and, most of all, by challenging men. Men and their habits, long outside the realm of female influence, seem to be a major concern of elected women.

Women are also aware that their strength comes not only from their numbers but also from their knowledge and skills, for example literacy. Thus, women see training as an important part of their empowerment. Many NGOs have seized on this as a fundamental issue and have begun to focus on the training of women. Clearly this is necessary, but the danger of too narrow a focus is to suggest that it is only women who need training. What the presence of women politicians has done is to invert the conventional hierarchies as to who are the teachers and who are the taught.

Such women are making it clear that it is the male extension officers who need training, and not just the female representatives. This is an important message for donors and other funders of training, who have tended to assume in the past that the objects of their support must be women. Women's empowerment challenges traditional ideas of male authority and supremacy. It is unsurprising, then, that PRI has been opposed by some men.

8

Rural Women Empowerment

Though the Constitutional commitments of the nation to women was translated through the planning process, legislation, policies and programmes over the last six decades yet as the Eleventh plan approaches, a situational analysis of social and economic status of women reflects less than satisfactory achievements in almost all important human development indicators. The maternal mortality rate is estimated at 407 per 100,000 live births in India compared to figures of 92 in Sri Lanka, 56 in China and 130 in Vietnam; the growing female face of HIV/AIDS is reflected in the fact that the number of pregnant women (between 18-24 years) with HIV prevalence comprise 0.86 per cent in 2003 of the total women pregnant compared to 0.74 per cent in 2002.

The saga of missing daughters is vividly depicted in the growing incidence of female foeticide as a result of which the child sex ratio has declined from 945 in 1991 to 927 in 2001. While the literacy rates have shown an improvement from 39.3 per cent to 54.3 per cent of the total female population between 1991 and 2001, yet much more needs to be done especially for socially and economically backward regions and groups.

Economic empowerment as reflected by the work participation rate shows that the percentage of women in the work force increased by only 3 per cent (from 22.5 per cent to 25.7 per cent) between 1991 and 2001. The average wage differential between men and women showed a marked deterioration between 2000 and 2004 for both rural and urban areas. The violence against women continued unabated with the absolute number of crimes against women increasing from 1,28,320 in 2000 to 1,43,615 in 2004.

With regard to the status of women in Indian society at large, no nation has held their women in higher esteem than the Hindus. Perhaps, no other literature has presented a more admirable type of woman character than Sita, Maitriya, Gargi. The Indian civilisation has produced great women ranging from Braham vadinis (lady Rishi) to states woman, from ideal wife to warrior queen. It dates back to thousands of years. Hindu mythology witnesses that the status of Hindu woman during the vedic period was honourable and respectable.

The marriage was regarded as sacrosanct and the family ideal was high. The woman on marriage acquired an honorable' position and considerable status. There are references, which indicate that, equal social and religious status was allowed to boys and girls in Vedic society. Boys and girls had equal opportunity for advanced education. The girls also spent early years of their life in brahamcharya ashram after observing Upanyana Sanskara for study of Vedas. It was thought necessary for girls otherwise automatically they would be reduced to status of Shudras. They could quit before recommended period of brahmacharya ashram as they were married at 16/17 years of age. They were then called Sadyovahas. If she continued her studies, she was called Brahmavadini.

Attainment of women in intellectual field is to be inferred from the fact that some of the hymns are attributed to female Rishis. They were on the same footing as men. They learnt the Vedas, were entitled to recite the Vedas and they were teachers as well as learners. They were poetesses, teachers and intellectuals of the day. Marriage was an established Institution in the Vedic Age. It was regarded as a social and religious duty-, it was not taken as a contract. The husband-wife stood on equal footing and prayed for long lasting love and friendship.

There was no tradition of child marriage prevailing in Vedic society. Wishes and choices of girls in the settlement of their marriage are also a strong indication of their status in society. The bride had the right of selecting her own consort. This custom was known as Svayamvara—Self-choice. Monogamy normally prevailed in Vedic age and this indicates high status of women in this period. Widows were allowed to remarry if they so desired.

In the Vedic era, women had sufficient freedom of going to attend fairs, festivals, and assemblies. They were not confined to four walls of their family houses. There is no mention of *Purdah* system. The strong cultural background of Indian society and high status of women kept them healthy from all perspectives—social, physical and psychological. During the post-vedic period, women started losing the status in society, which she attained in the Vedic age. She lost her independence. She became a subject of protection. Manu, the progenitor of Hindu race, stated that a woman should be kept day and night in subordination by males of the family—woman has to be protected by her father in childhood, by her husband in young age and by the sons in old age. She lost her identity after marriage.

Manu's codes are legal authority of the time with respect to Hindu family. He regards daughters as an object of highest tenderness. He did not treat women at par with man so far as rituals of Vedas are concerned. The woman was not eligible for the study of Vedas, nor for use of mantras in performing sacraments except marriage. Serving to husband is equivalent to living in the house of teacher, household duties amount to yagna for her. Manu believed that there is vital structural difference between man and woman, each suited for different type of work. He regards women as more emotional and less rational by nature than man; does not possess much depth of reason.

Man was responsible for hard work, earning the bread and women for household duties. Manu says, "when creating them, God allotted to woman a love of their bed, of their seat, and of ornaments, impure desires, wrath, dishonesty, mature and bad conduct. That is why Manu does not contemplate equality between man and woman in different walks of life. He has however, made contradictory statements. At one point, Manu has said, "Woman should be honoured and adored by fathers and brothers, by husbands and also by brother-in-law. Where women are honoured the Gods rejoice, but when they are neglected, all rites and ceremonies are fruitless".

Women were preordained for procreation and they had no other function. Manu was of the opinion that women do not need any education. Marriage of girls forms their Initiation into study of Vedas. Marriages were settled soon after puberty. The institution of caste became very rigid with strict hierarchical gradations. Brahmanical order was firmly established. Manu did not favour inter-caste marriages.

Polygamy and Monogamy was prevalent. Brahmans could possess 3 wives, Kshatriyas - 2, Vaishyas - 1 besides 1 Shudra wife for all, only for pleasure and not for religious rites. Evidences of widow remarriage during this period are conflicting; there are cases of permission as well as of prohibition. A widow was generally not allowed to remarry. Women were incapable of possessing property.

Manu regards the wife as the half of her husband though not better half. According to Manu, man does not make a whole by himself alone but attains completion in the company of his wife. Manu wanted that women should not only be honoured, she should not be put to any grief. However, he insisted that a husband should be constantly worshipped (even if he was not a ideal husband) as God by a faithful wife. By violating her duty towards her husband, a wife is disgraced in this world or is tormented by diseases as punishment for her sin. The birth of a son has been very important from worldly, religious and spiritual point of view. Birth of a son was necessary to pay off the debt to ancestors. *Putra* signifies one who saves a person from hell.

During the Moghul rule, the socio-economic status of Hindu women were very much lowered and had to depend on the Hindu male in every activity. The social evils like *Purdah* system came into force. Child marriage was prevalent. Lack of education, early marriage, nonexistence of employment opportunities, absence of absolute property rights were main causes of inequality of sex in the socio-economic field. Economic dependence made a Hindu Woman socially backward. Incidence of female infanticide and custom of Sati could be witnessed. The women came to be regarded as of the same status as the Sudras. Girls were to get married before puberty; the age of 8 was regarded as ideal. Early marriage was followed by early maternity, which increased mortality among women.

During the British rule in India, legislation was used to bring about significant modifications in the structure society. Various reforms were initiated with respect to status of women. Free India has carried forward the process to a point where legally at least men and women are equal. However, some of the basic cultural orientations towards men and women in contemporary Indian society have been shaped by the authority of classical texts, teachings of religion, factors of historical development and the persistence of regional and local traditions.

The contradictory attitudes expressed about women in classical texts persist in contemporary society. On the one hand, they are regarded as the highest embodiment of purity and power—a symbol of religiousness and spirituality, on the other; they are viewed essentially as weak and dependent creatures requiring constant guidance and protection. While girls are also considered necessary, the birth of a boy has been considered more desirable.

Ritual considerations materially add to the desirability of the male. In the traditional scheme of Hindu life, the attainment of salvation occupies the place of highest importance. For this it is necessary to complete all the rites ceremonies of the life cycle prescribed by dharma. In the patrilineal Hindu society, only a male can offer water to the spirits of the deceased ancestors; a son alone can perform the essential rites ensuring passage to heaven or attainment of salvation. This makes a male offspring very desirable.

It is believed, parents can depend on sons for support in old age and are looked upon as potential builders of family prestige and prosperity. On the contrary, daughters are considered to be destined for others, their upbringing is all worry and work for the parents. The difficulties and expenses involved in her upbringing and marriage further detract from her desirability. Even today in a large number of Hindu households, the birth of son is an occasion for rejoicing; the birth of a daughter is a cause for anxiety.

The assumption of superiority of males has built up the ideas of male dominance and female dependence. Most of the major decisions-making roles are thus the domain of man in most cases. These cultural attributes have left a deep mark on women's development in India; of-course it varies according to specific variables operating in Indian society such as caste, class, rural, urban, education, region and other socio-economic parameters.

In India, outside the educated elite and often even within it, girls are considered an economic liability because of the tradition that requires a girl's parents to provide her with a dowry at the time of her marriage. Indian society has had a culture of *Kanyadan* and *Varadakshina* where the parents offer their daughter to the bridegroom and give affectionate gifts in kind or cash with the intention of setting up the household of the new couple at the start of their life together.

Also there has been the notion of *streedhan,* which relates to the ornaments given to the bride by her father or brother, the intention, again being to help the daughter to tide over difficulties, if ever the situation so warranted. Over a period of time these cultural attributes became a compulsion and the whole process has been commercialised. For many families, the dowry represents an enormous financial burden. The dowry system is directly linked to many harmful practices against women and girls in India, including burning of brides over dowry disputes.

Because of the perception that girls are a drain on family resources, in some cases i.e. depending on the socio-economic parameters, families are unwilling to invest in daughters. Male children are breastfed longer and receive more and better food and more timely and costly healthcare than their female siblings. Girls with older sisters appear at a particular disadvantage. Higher childhood mortality among girls is primarily responsible for the skewed sex ratio in the Indian population. The sex ratio varies greatly on a state-by-state basis, which reflects differences in female literacy and other indicators of women's status.

Female infanticide and female foeticide play a substantial role in the lop sided sex ratio in India. Poor families in certain regions sometimes resort to killing baby girls at birth-usually second and subsequent daughters—to avoid an unwanted burden on family resources. Sex selective abortion has also been common. Amniocentesis, a technology to detect any foetal abnormality, has been used for determining the sex of fetus and the selective abortion of female fetuses has been widespread cutting across various societal parameters.

Higher levels of female education are strongly related to increased age at marriage, knowledge and practice of contraception and smaller family size. Culturally, Goddess of learning Saraswati is revered and worshipped by all in the society but families from lower socio-economic group are often reluctant to Invest in their daughter's education. Literacy remains low among women compared to men.

The gender gap in education is far greater in the northern states. Even in states where enrolment rates for girls are higher, many girls drop out of school after only a few years of education. Cultural factors such as inhibition on education being imparted by male teachers to girls once they reach puberty, is responsible for drop-outs. Early marriage and childbirth continue to be the social norm in India, these cultural compulsions are more pronounced in families of lower socio-economic status though sometimes middle class families reflect the same phenomena.

Within the context of specific variables such as socio-economic status, caste, tribal group, region, education and such differentials, after marriage, a woman is under the authority of her mother-in-law and generally has little autonomy in decision making, even regarding her own fertility. Some of them live in physical seclusion or *Purdah*. Their isolation and limited freedom of movement contribute to their dependence and restrict their access to family planning information and services.

Women derive their status primarily from their child bearing role and their value is often measured by the number of sons they have. Women themselves depend on male children for social status and economic security and are often reluctant to use contraception prior to having a son. Family planning practice rises significantly among women who have two or more sons. The cultural practice of woman eating last in the family takes a toll on her health if it is a household of low economic status.

The most direct effects of poor health and nutrition among females in Indian society are high mortality rates among young children and women of child bearing age and morbidity rates throughout the life cycle. The effects of pervasive ill health extend beyond the woman herself. A woman's health and nutritional status influence her newborn's birth weight and chances of survival, her capacity to nurse and nurture her child and her ability to provide food and care for the family members.

Post neo-natal deaths are generally caused by infectious diseases. The incidence and severity of most of these diseases are affected by controllable factors such as immunisation, health care and nutrition. Where gender bias exists, these factors are not controlled equally for male and female children. Maternal mortality in India estimated at 437 maternal deaths per 100,000 live births, results primarily from infection, haemorrhage, obstructed labour, abortion and anaemia. Lack of appropriate care during pregnancy and childbirth, utilising the services of Dais or untrained midwives, lack of motivation on part of family members to take medical advice from doctors for the women in question, explain most of the maternal deaths.

SOCIAL EMPOWERMENT OF WOMEN

The Tenth Five Year Plan categorised the developmental needs of the female population using the tool of age and classified them into five age-groups.

— Girls in the age group of 0-14,
— Adolescent girls in the age group of 15-19,
— Women in the reproductive age group of 19 to 44,
— Women in the economically active age group of 45 to 59,
— Older women in the age group of 60 + and above.

The first two categories comprising infants, children and young girls represent roughly half of the country's female population. Within these two categories, there are especially defenceless subgroups, such as the girl children of tender years, when discrimination in matters such as food intake, health and medical care, schooling, recreational facilities etc. is entrenched both within families as well as communities as well as larger social formations. Another group consists of girls stepping from childhood to adolescence, facing a new grown-up world, with very little preparation of learning, knowledge or skills, or of how to come to terms with their own emerging sexuality in a patriarchal environment.

While age is an important marker in categorising women, there is also the necessity of looking at other criteria such as those based on certain socio-economic differentials. Besides looking into women, on the whole, as a discriminated lot, it is important to reflect on the reality that women are not a homogeneous category. The draft Approach Paper to the Eleventh Plan repeatedly emphasises the need to restructure growth as a broad and inclusive process. It frankly admits that even the achievement of reaching broad based and inclusive growth will not suffice to reach "certain marginalised groups' and that the 11th Plan must pay special attention to the needs of these groups. The Paper points to SC's, ST's, some OBC's and minorities as those who are lagging behind. The women and girls belonging to such groups are doubly disadvantaged and, therefore, need more attention in the XI Plan.

In fact, viewing women as a distinctly separate group (from men) misses out the intersections between gender and other variables of social and economic status. These intersections reinforce vulnerability of more than one type and result in double and triple discrimination amongst women belonging to these groups. It is necessary not only to unravel these threads and trace several distinctive roots of inequality and discrimination, but also to conceive of multi-layered responses in planning and programming in order to bridge the divides using the theme of 'inclusive growth'. "While gender is undoubtedly an independent source of vulnerability, what is of particular concern is the way class, social and gender relationships reinforce one another in order to increase the insecurity and vulnerability of poor, low caste women" Srivastava.

The proposition is that there is a certain predisposition to being deprived of human development opportunities, even where these opportunities, state provided or otherwise, exist for the men and women of these communities. What is less recognised is that this predisposition is aggravated in the case of women of these communities—being a woman exacerbates the conditions of being poor, illiterate, landless, asset-less and (or) suffering from poor health morbidity or malnutrition. This systemic differentiation has to be responded to using the enabling provisions of Article 15(3) in respect of women of these deprived groups. Extending this beyond (but inclusive of) the gender logic, it is possible to draw inferences that there are as glaring disparities between women and girls of different social and economic groups as there are between men and women (including girls) of different groups.

Women from Minority Community

The main issues of Muslim minority women stem from three major factors:

— insecurity,

— exclusion, and

— poverty.

Effect of disaster

Experiences have shown that disaster, however 'natural', is profoundly discriminatory. Wherever they hit, preexisting structures and social conditions determine that some members of the community will pay a higher price. Among the differences that determine how people are affected by such disasters is that of gender.

Women's lower status in general results in various kinds of exclusions and vulnerabilities in a disaster setting. Low mobility and lower access to information implies that women are often the last to receive relief resources. Women are disproportionately represented within the informal and agricultural sectors, which are the most adversely affected by disasters. This adversely affects their claim to relief and rehabilitation. Thus, women experience high rates of unemployment, even further decreasing their bargaining power within households and communities. Unlike men, they are the primary household caretakers and thus are not able to migrate for work. All these factors involving structural biases and gender discrimination results in the compensation amounts awarded being directed invariably at men.

Disasters create the potential to engage in longer-term rights and equity-based development through critical and practical strategies for gender empowerment. Successfully incorporating women within disaster management and mitigation is one way to increase women's social, political and economic status in general, and to minimise the currently disproportionate impact of disasters on women. Strategies include strengthening the marketable skills of women, promoting livelihood options, enhancing women's leadership in micro-planning, relief and disaster mitigation and increasing their role in local governance.

Practically, women have immense knowledge of their local environments and information about how to mitigate risks that lead to disasters. This knowledge can be transformed into actionable expertise by involving women within disaster management.

Women in the North-East

The conflict situation in the North-East is rooted in lack of income and employment. The Look East policy of the GOI could be a valuable device to open opportunities. Of special attention are issues related to introducing new avenues for non-farming activities of women—food processing, bottling, canning and packaging. Attention needs to be paid to creating job oriented skills for manufacture of indigenous products, popularising indigenous cuisine in the potential tourist areas and highways, skills in hotel management, creating travel guides to depict north-east histories, cultures and traditional assets etc.

Women are the most vulnerable section of society in Border trade centres and areas, which are adjacent to international borders and normally a 'no-man's land' controlled by antisocial elements and organisations that are inimical to the interests of the country. Under the circumstances, women, who are the major component in border trades, especially in agriculture and allied activities, are under severe threat. Matters are compounded by problems of infrastructure and facilities, which are either most rudimentary or simply do not exist. Access to health, education, drinking water, and sanitation, etc, is almost impossible, which adversely affect health.

Border Trade Centres/Areas besides normally being hot beds of smuggling, particularly of narcotics, also are centres of trafficking of women and children. Women are rendered vulnerable to all kinds of diseases, especially STD, HIV/AIDS. Women are also used or forced into smuggling of narçotics, which makes them further vulnerable to law-enforcing agencies that are not sensitised to dealing with women lawbreakers. The circle gets more vicious for women in these areas, many of whom are either illiterate or have received only rudimentary education and cannot be expected to be aware of their fundamental, human, legal and other rights. Problems of communication, organised marketing and non-implementation of labour laws also adversely affect women's economic power, which in turn reinforces them to play subservient roles and their empowerment continues to remain illusionary and elusive.

It is therefore suggested that some mechanism is set-up in Border Trade Centres and Areas to enforce the law of the land, as also to implement and monitor all fundamental, human, legal and other rights to ensure that no citizen of this country is denied and deprived of them. Enhancing the utilisation of the region's local and rich natural resources with appropriate technology for producing and marketing herbal products and processed food/fruits is another avenue to meet with the challenge posed by antisocial elements. Cold storages can be located in appropriate areas of the region, to sustain perishable items before they are transported to larger markets.

Urban Poor

Urbanisation is an increasing phenomenon as the nature of activities pursued by an economy progressively shifts from primary to the secondary and tertiary sectors. Urban poor settlements in India are around 40 million and the average family size is 5. It has been projected by the Planning commission (Working group on 9th Plan) that by the end of the 9th Plan and at the beginning of the 10th Plan, the shortage of housing in urban areas would be 16.76 million houses. Of this 10 million houses would be needed for the economically weaker sections, which can be broadly categorised as below poverty line population.

- — Women's rights to housing need to be understood in terms of their entitlements. This means they have rights in, access to and control over land, housing and property. The state must evolve policies and programmes that are sensitive to the nuances of women's status-linked needs—aged, widows, divorced, and single.
- — There is a need for greater commitment to institutional re-orientation by adopting a more 'enabling' approach to the delivery of basic services accessible to the poor through the more effective mobilisation of community resources and skills to compliment public resource allocations.

— Major areas of attention include: town planning, land management, adequate housing, poverty alleviation, and provision of basic amenities, access to social services such as health, education, access to credit etc. all of which are crucial for women's human capital development and for reducing the incidence of poverty.

— Improved access to social services would also help in building up the capacities of poor women and empowering them to improve their own living conditions and quality of life.

— Effective delivery of these services would also reduce social and gender inequities and promote integration of people residing in slums into the social and economic networks of the city as a whole, thereby enhancing the overall productivity of the city.

— Various physical infrastructure components such as water supply and sanitation have a direct bearing on improving health conditions in slums, especially of women.

— There is a need for formulating a National Urban Settlements for the Poor Policy, which would cover the above said components. Women's needs arising from their gendered position as well as their being poor, should form part of the policy.

Social Empowerment

Women and girls in India face a crisis of growing, yet un-addressed, health needs. From the moment of conception to the end of life, the challenges to the female sex are enormous, especially poor women who have limited access to health care. The child sex ratio continues to plummet and is as low as 793 in an economically prosperous and progressive state such as Punjab.

Malnutrition begins during infancy and sets in motion a life-long cycle of poor health. Over half of all Indian women suffer from anaemia, which acerbates maternal morbidity. More women die of maternal death related causes in India than in any other country in the world. While NACO data highlights that many new HIV cases are of married women, the National Family Health Survey, 1998-99 shows that only four out of ten women in the reproductive age have heard of HIV/AIDS.

Despite the alarming health crisis of women and girls, the national policy focus prioritises family planning and reproductive health without addressing underlying issues such as women's low participation in decision-making, which adversely affects her health status. Another important point to note is that the leading killer of women in India is tuberculosis. Yet due to the focus on maternal and reproductive health this fact is little known nor are there any gender specific policies or programmes in place with regard to this disease.

Violence as a public health issue

NFHS-2 shows disturbing evidence that women have internalised domestic violence as a necessary part of domestic marital relationships. More than half of all Indian women believe that husbands can beat wives if they have an appropriate reason for doing so. Half of non-working married women in India don't make personal healthcare decisions, almost three-fourths (72 per cent) need permission to go to the market and just over one-tenth (11 per cent) are not involved in any household decisions at all. Violence, neglect and abuse not only result in long-term physical injuries and poor health, but also create chronic low-self-esteem, depression and other mental health issues for women. Despite the high rate of violence against women, including neglect, rape, dowry murder and domestic violence, violence is not seen as a public health issue.

Low budgetary allocation

Despite the health crisis of women and girls, India is consistently among the lowest of all countries in terms of its investment in health, as acknowledged in the National Health Policy of 2002. India's investment in health as a proportion of GDP has vacillated from 1.3 per cent in 1990 to .9 in 2001, making it amongst the lowest global spenders on health. In 2002, India's public health expenditure as a proportion of GDP rose to 1.3 per cent A great deal of rural indebtedness in poor rural families is linked to rising health costs. The importance of public provisioning of quality health care to enable access to affordable and reliable health services cannot be overestimated in the context of preventing the non-poor from entering into poverty or in terms of reducing the suffering of those who are already below the poverty line.

Low investment in health and the under-utilisation of funds has resulted in health delivery systems that are increasingly inaccessible, inefficient and unaffordable. Currently, little investment is made on front-line public health care workers, who have extensive workloads, multiple areas of responsibility and multiple lines of accountability with little compensation.

Healthcare access

Health care access remains low for many women, especially those who are poor; suffer from multiple exclusions, including caste, class, geographic isolation and tribal status. Health policies have few specific strategies for improving access to marginalised groups.

— Specific IEC and training strategies should be developed in all programmes to target excluded groups, including tribal and low-caste communities.

— Ensure women-friendly free comprehensive primary health care, based on a life cycle approach, with full preventive, curative and promotive care at the PHC level with free ambulance referral and/or alternate transport mechanism by identifying a pool of transport in the local area and reimbursement by the State.

— Integrate grievance cell and help lines with health services to ensure speedy investigation and facilitate redressal for users and health workers. Set up special counters in all health centres and easy referrals for improving access to free comprehensive health care particularly for stigmatised groups such as sex workers, hijras etc.

— Ensure access to women with disabilities through provision of ramps, lifts in public offices, transport etc and provide rehab and equipment (wheelchair, hearing aids etc) as a right.

Reproductive health: The high rates of MMR and IMR, poor pre natal and post natal care combined with the low proportion of institutional deliveries is a grave cause of concern. Therefore the reproductive health care of women needs special attention in the XI Plan. For this purpose:

— Ensure full enforcement of Supreme Court guidelines on sterilisation.

— The current policy focus on female sterilisation should be broadened to providing people with greater reproductive choice. This includes better access to contraception, more information about birth spacing, increasing male responsibility for small families, as well as providing greater education and economic opportunities for women.

— Reproductive and maternal health programmes, including RCH, should not be combined with the goals and strategies of population stabilisation.

— The NPP, Health plan and NRHM policy documents must include institutionalised mechanisms and for ensuring that states comply with the no-target policy of the national government. This includes preventing states from denying women participation on the PRI, or accessing other benefits for having more than two children.

— Policies should promote strategies for involving men that foster equitable gender relationships. This includes equitable decision-making and resource-sharing amongst couples how men can take more responsibility for birth control and foster greater opportunities for their wives/daughters.

— Policies should address how women's non-reproductive health status impacts reproductive health. This includes understanding trends in how TB, malaria and HIV interact with one another and impact women's maternal health.

— Ensure a clearly defined package of essential Reproductive health services including ante and post natal care, emergency Obstetric care, information about and services for contraception and safe abortion and counselling at the PHC, free to all women and adolescents (married or unmarried).

— The Janani Suraksha Yojana should be extended to cover all poor women irrespective of their age, parity, or place of childbirth.

— Extend maternity leave to 6 months and provide maternity benefits for ALL women of all sections irrespective of the parity.

— Ensure regular collection of data on maternal morbidity and mortality (as done with fertility and demographic data through the NFHS and DLHS), to facilitate decentralised planning and monitoring as envisaged within the NRHM.

— Provide adequately trained attendance at delivery-at home or in institutions, with emergency referral backup and a continuum of care from pregnancy through childbirth and 42 days hence.

— Recognise the role of traditional birth attendants and upgrade their skills.

— The health insurance schemes being implemented by government and private sector should also cover the pregnancy period (both normal and caesarian cases). The premium of these schemes should be kept to the minimum so that the poor women can have access to these schemes.

Mental Health: Ensure availability of required mental health professionals, psychiatrist, psychologist, psychiatric social worker, and mental health nurses at all levels. Undertake periodic assessment of treatment facilities including rehabilitation at district level. Develop a National Policy on Mental Health with adequate budget provision at both Centre and State level.

POLITICAL EMPOWERMENT OF WOMEN

The National Common Minimum Programme lays down empowerment of women politically, educationally and legally as one of the six basic principles. To provide an impetus to this objective, the Finance Minister in the budget speech for 2004-05 highlighted the perceived need for budget data to be presented in a manner that highlights the gender sensitiveness of the budgetary allocations. This was followed by a more emphatic commitment in the budget speech of 2005-06, wherein the budgetary allocations under 10 demand for grants estimated at Rs. 14379 crore were highlighted in a separate statement as a part of the Gender Budgeting exercise. The 2006-07 Budget Speech revealed an estimated allocation of Rs. 28,737 cr. for benefit of women under 24 demand for grants in 18 Ministries and Departments.

In spite of these commitments and focus on women's development and empowerment, the present status of women continues to be quite dismal in terms of important human development parameters like health, nutrition, literacy, educational attainments, skill levels, occupational status etc. There are a number of gender specific barriers, which prevent women for gaining access to their rightful share in the flow of public goods and services. Unless the felt needs of women are incorporated and mainstreamed in the planning and development process it is apprehended that the fruits of economic growth are likely to completely bypass a significant section of the country's population which does not augur well for the future growth of the economy. This calls for a focused priority in the Eleventh plan for the strengthening, expansion and universalisation of Gender Budgeting in all its aspects.

Gender Budgeting

Gender Budgeting is defined as the application of gender mainstreaming in the budgetary process. It encompasses incorporating a gender perspective at all levels and stages of the budgetary process and paves the way for translating gender commitments to budgetary commitments and carrying out an assessment of the budget to establish its gender differential impact.

In other words Gender Budgeting looks at Government budget from a gender perspective to assess how it addresses the needs of women not only in traditional areas like health, education etc., but also in so called 'gender neutral' sectors like Transport, Power, Telecommunications, Defence etc. It does not seek to create a separate budget but seeks to put in place affirmative action for meeting women's specific needs, thus bringing into effect gender responsive Budgeting. The ultimate objective of gender budgeting is to transform and transcend traditional perceptions and mind sets towards women and awaken a gender sensitive consciousness which will not only enable women to come into the mainstream but also give them their due recognition as equal citizens of the country.

The Ministry of Women and Child Development (MWCD) in 2004-05 adopted the mission statement of 'Budgeting for Gender Equity'. In 2005-06 the task was to carry forward this exercise of universalising gender budgeting exercises in the Centre and the States. Several initiatives have been undertaken by MWCD to operationalise Gender Budgeting. A strategic framework of activities to implement "Budgeting for Gender Equity" disseminated to all Departments identifies areas for gender mainstreaming including quantification of allocation of resources for women in Union/ State/ Local Budgets, gender audit of polices of Governments, impact assessment of various schemes, analysing programmes and strategies, institutionalising generation and collection of gender desegregated data, consultations and capacity building etc.

Further, guidelines for gender sensitive review of public expenditure and policy were framed in the form of checklists both for beneficiary oriented sectors (such as Health, Rural Development, Human Resource Development, Labour, Drinking Water, Textiles, Agriculture etc.) and for mainstream sectors that may appear "gender neutral" like defence, power, telecom, transport etc. The Ministry has conducted several workshops and training programmes to disseminate the tools of gender budgeting and has advocated that a review may be undertaken with respect to

— Gender Based Profile of Public expenditure,
— Beneficiary needs assessment,
— Impact Analysis,
— Participative Budgeting, and
— Spatial Mapping.

The MWCD has requested Ministries to set up Gender Budgeting Cells to undertake review of the public expenditure and policy, guide and undertake collection of gender desegregated data, conduct gender based impact analysis, beneficiary needs assessment and beneficiary incidence analysis. As a result of these efforts 43 Ministries/Departments have set up Gender Budget Cells as a nodal agency for all gender responsive budgeting initiatives.

Women's Component Plan (WCP)

The WCP was the first major initiative taken by the Government to address women related issues and requirements on a systematic basis involving the inputs from major Ministries/Departments. The Women's Component Plan (WCP) involved efforts to ensure that not less than 30 per cent of funds/benefits were earmarked for women under the various schemes. However, performance on the WCP has been disappointing and the Mid Term Appraisal of the Tenth Plan notes that while "the Department of Education has confirmed a flow of funds of 42.37 per cent of the gross budgetary support to the WCP, the Ministry of Labour, which had reported flow of 33.5 per cent of its budget to the WCP in the Ninth Plan, has reported flow of funds of only 5 per cent of its budget during first three years of Tenth Plan." Several Ministries and/or Departments, which had earlier reported on the WCP in their sectorial budgets, have stopped doing so.

It also noted that there are some Ministries and Departments, which have the potential to go beyond 30 per cent of funds under WCP as well as devise and administer women related programmes. These include Education, Health, Family Welfare, Environment and Forests, Rural Development, Agriculture, Labour, Urban Affairs, Drinking Water Supply, Tribal Affairs, Social Justice and Empowerment, and possibly others. It also pointed out that the Ministries and Departments "that have defaulted in providing WCP allocations or whose WCP is less than 30 per cent of their budgets are advised to immediately take the necessary steps to make amends."

Taking the essence and intent of the Mid term appraisal of the Tenth plan, WCP would need to be extended to all Ministries and Departments and not confined to the realm of some Ministries and Departments which have historically been perceived as "women-related". Simultaneously the implementation process of Gender Budgeting needs to be institutionalised and universalised in all the Ministries/ Departments at the Centre and States.

Vision of gender budgeting

With the objective of gender mainstreaming as the ultimate aim, Gender Budgeting seeks to truly empower woman in every respect and enable her to realise her full potential in all spheres—political, economic, social, cultural and civil. Towards this end Gender Budgeting helps ensure better access of women to health and education facilities, vocational training, employment opportunity and social security etc. for women. Setting up functional Gender Budgeting Cells in all Ministries/ Departments in the Centre and the States with a view to mainstream gender concerns in all areas of Government is therefore vital and needs to be taken up on a priority basis.

Gender Budgeting cannot be restricted only to government programmes and schemes. If it is to be truly successful and beneficial to women, the process has to permeate and penetrate to all sectors, policies and strategies and reach out to all sections of the governance and the community. Only then can gender budgeting completely fulfil its objective of truly empowering women keeping in view this macro vision of gender budgeting the recommendations for the Eleventh plan are as follows:

National macro-economic policies: Policies of the Government form the genesis for programmes and schemes providing the direction and describing the components of inputs that go into them. They determine the quantum of flow of the funds to different schemes, its components and also spatial spread of the programme. Unless the policies are engendered, it cannot be hoped that the programmes and the schemes that emerge from this will be gender sensitive. Therefore, it is very essential that all policies of the Government from its very inception and formulation stage be thoroughly examined from a gender perspective. The following paragraphs indicate the various possibilities and potential of engendering some important national policies.

The fiscal and monetary policies: Fiscal and monetary policies will need to be analysed from a gender perspective as both have tremendous potential to have malefic or benign influence on the lives of women. Indirect taxation impinges heavily on women as the tax incidence, by and large, affects important items of sustenance which are generally highly price inelastic and even a small price rise in such items will have a negative impact on women; again the subsidy needs a re-look to ensure that withdrawal of subsidies do not adversely impinge on women. For example, withdrawal of subsidy on kerosene with no other alternative fuel options will result in the woman wasting valuable productive time in gathering firewood, twigs etc and in the process also face health hazards. Thus the ramifications of indirect taxes are quite significant as far as women's well being is considered. The gender affirmative role of direct taxation could be further enhanced through various incentives like reduction in stamp duties for women if assets are registered in their name, lowering of income tax slabs for women etc.

Monetary policy: Monetary policy has to be viewed from a gender angle, especially in the case of credit and loan facilities and easy access of women to financial instruments and attractive saving options. In this context the spread of private micro credit lending instruments needs to be carefully regulated to ensure that women and SHGs are not exploited through high interest rates.

Agricultural policies: Agricultural policies are of prime importance in gender budgeting exercises as there is a growing feminisation of agriculture in recent years without migration of men moving to urban areas in search of work. It is estimated that 75 per cent of all female workers and 85 per cent of all rural female workers are in agriculture. Women constitute 40 per cent of the agriculture force and this percentage is rising. The number of women headed households in the agricultural sector is also increasing. The prosperity of agriculture therefore will largely depend on how effectively these women are empowered.

Enhancing women's' rights to land, providing infrastructure support to women farmers and advancing legal support on existing laws are some of the policy interventions needed. However, critical problems persist. The lack of formal titles to women on the land they cultivate is a big drawback. This adversely affects their access to credit, inputs and marketing outlets. It also reinforces the woman's position as unpaid farm labour which reduces their incentives to invest in the land. It further excludes them from receiving services of agricultural extension services, new production techniques etc. The lack of appropriate women friendly tools and agricultural implements is another drawback. Also the farmers' cooperatives basically comprise of men and therefore disadvantageous to women in terms of mind set and location and services profile. The agricultural policy will therefore need to be reviewed to provide a gender friendly perspective.

Policies for the *Non-farm sector and information* is another highly important area that has to seriously reviewed keeping in view the gender perspective. As women tend to remain in the rural sector they also undertake non-farm activities, which significantly contributed to the family's income. In times of agricultural stress, it is these non-farm activities of women that support the family. Therefore, the requirements of women in this sector needs to be identified and appropriate support facilities in terms of access to raw materials, micro credit, skill development, training, market linkages etc. have to be ensured.

Poverty alleviation programmes should essentially focus on women as they are economically more disadvantaged than men and chronically poor. These alleviation programmes should be geared and designed to meet women's needs with strengthening of SHGs, easy access to cheap credit, equal wages for equal work and a judicious mix of cash and non cash in the wages etc. With the advent of mega poverty alleviation schemes like the National Rural Employment Guarantee Scheme, more and more women are coming forward to work. It is important that the work place should be made safe from harassment and woman friendly with adequate provision of sanitation, drinking water and creche facilities.

The existing *public distribution system* has failed to deliver the required food grains to the vulnerable groups on time in the requisite quality and quantity. The persisting problems of under weight, malnutrition, anaemia are primary causes for early mortality, morbidity, high rates of MMR etc. There is urgent need to review and streamline the policy and strategy of PDS to ensure easy and timely distribution of food grains to women. The institution of food/grain banks and managing the same by women SHGs could be considered to enable uninterrupted supply of food grains even in times of drought or other natural/man-made disasters.

Public policy with respect to *migration* is another area for consideration. Due to extreme poverty or seasonal farm work, women are forced to migrate to semi urban / urban areas. There are large numbers of social and economic consequences, which these women face such as exploitation in work place, wages differentials, low paid work etc. Also their access to safe housing, food, sanitation and health remain precarious. A very alarming feature of unregulated migration is the trafficking of young girls and women by duping, luring or kidnapping them. Such women are forced into prostitution, bonded labour or slavery. These social aspects need to be looked into in greater detail while reviewing the *Migration policy.*

The possibilities of gender differentials for social security *insurance* schemes is another area that need to be examined, as there is an urgent need for low cost and gender friendly insurance systems that cater to the specific life-cycle needs of women. It must be acknowledged that a safety net/social security in the informal sector is almost non existent. As women comprise a large proportion of the informal sector, this implies that they are excluded from the insurance framework and therefore not protected against social, medical or economic emergencies. More importantly, it is absolutely necessary to put in place a well designed *Health Insurance* scheme for women in view of their inability to access medical facilities. Also pensions policy needs a relook in view of the large number of widow population in the country.

Environmental concerns also warrant gender mainstreaming. Providing alternative sources of fuel for women especially in rural areas reduces both her drudgery with collection of firewood and exposure to pollutants; switching from fossil fuel to non conventional fuel based systems such as green fuels (bio-mass), solar power, hydel power etc. should be stressed. Women's SHGs should be encouraged to be actively involved in Watershed Committees, Joint Forest Management Committees etc. There is a double advantage from this exercise, as on the one hand environment preservation issues will be addressed and on the other women will be empowered.

Disaster management policy should become gender sensitive as experiences have shown that women are most affected by disasters whether manmade or natural. The tendency for trafficking, sale of women and children is quite common in these extenuating circumstances. The emergency response systems in the event of such disasters should have well thought out gender relief measures to cater to afflicted women and children without any delay.

Media policy needs to be gender proactive. There is a need to encourage media to project positive images and balanced portrayal of women and girls to enable attitudinal changes. The media policy should also help in generating awareness on gender issues and concerns so that the process of societal reorientation towards creating a gender just society gets widely disseminated.

Research and Development should also be geared with a view to identify technological needs of women and develop and adapt technology especially to reduce the drudgery of women, facilitating her health and also income generating activities. The Information Technology Policy should also be women oriented imparting skills and strengthening the knowledge base of girls and women in the field of computer software and hardware especially in rural areas. Dissemination of information in local languages on socio-economic and legal issues concerning women would encourage better awareness and instill confidence. Information Technology Kiosks need to be opened for women which would facilitate the Self Help Groups in using internet facilities to purchase raw material designing and marketing of their products.

The above is an illustrative list of engendering national policies. Similar gender perspectives and mainstreaming has to be built into all policies whether they are economic, social or political in nature as Gender Budgeting cannot be seen in isolation from the overall socio-economic-political scenario. The successful impact of these policies on women implies the successful implementation of Gender Budgeting.

While the gender sensitisation of policies, programmes and schemes go a long way in empowering women, it is human development indicators, which reflect the ultimate and true empowerment of women in the country. In a way, these indicators are the outcomes of the gender budgeting, yet in their own sphere they are also the process inputs for gender budgeting.

Unfortunately, the basic parameters of health, nutrition, education, employment and training reflect the continuing dismal status of women in the country. While individual sectorial policies, be it health, education, employment etc. will be separately engendered, cross cutting holistic intersectoral policies also need to be converged effectively with a gender perspective, if Human Development Indicies are to improve. Therefore along with sectorial polices, intersectoral polices too need to be gendered defined.

The laws and legalisation are the framework that provide women her rights as equal citizens of the country. There are over 42 women specific and related legislations. Some women specific legislations include the Immoral Traffic (Prevention) Act 1956, Maternity Benefit Act 1961, Dowry Prohibition Act 1961, Protection of Women from Domestic Violence Act 2005 etc which seek to protect the women from sexual exploitation and other violence and abuse; women related legislations which have economic implications include the Factories Act 1948, Minimum Wages Act 1948, Equal Remuneration Act, 1976 etc, many of which have provisions for providing economic justice and fair wages to women; there are other Acts which are Protection oriented such as Pre-conception and Prenatal Diagnostic Techniqu Regulation and Prevention) Act 1994, Child Marriage Restraint Act 1929; and those with Social implications like Family Courts Act 1984, Hindu Succession 1956, Indian Divorce Act 1969.

Thus while there are a plethora of Acts existing for the protection and socio-economic equality of women, it is only through their effective implementation that women receive the intended benefits. However, gaps still remain and it is essential that specific laws are brought into effect which provide adequate safeguards and protection to women. One such very important Act is the Compulsory Registration of Marriage Act, which will protect the marital rights of the women and ensure her rightful share in the husband's property.

While the planning process and public expenditure in terms of programmes and schemes are sought to be included in Gender Budgeting, yet without gender sensitivity of important organs such as police, judiciary etc., the implementation will not be successful. This is especially true of such schemes which have a strong element of protection or are rights based. For example, if the woman is not given her due share of property or other assets as per law it is essential that these agencies help and support her in getting her share without much delay or harassment.

This can happen only if gender sensitivity is inculcated in such bodies, and they are made aware of the laws, policies, programmes and other initiatives for women. It is also important that justice delivery is quick with the enforcement machinery being responsive and gender sensitive to women's needs especially in cases of domestic violence and personal assault.

A very effective method of ensuring that gender concerns are not lost sight of in such bodies is the induction of larger number of women at different levels. This will encourage women to actively participate in power sharing and active participation in decision-making. Efforts should be made to provide coaching facilities and support services so that women can compete along with men both at entry and to facilitate upward mobility of women in these institutions.

The setting up of "women" police stations, women's help desk in every police station, and increasing the strength of women police to 30 per cent of the total force has been reiterated a number of times by the Ministry of Women and Child Development in a number of forums. The Ministry of Home Affairs should take requisite steps to fulfil their obligations towards gender budgeting by 'engendering the police force'.

While so far the focus of gender budgeting has been on public expenditure of Government only, an increasing quantum of funds is being invested by the corporate sector in their businesses as well as in fulfilling their corporate social responsibility.

The development of the corporate sector as an employer has grown tremendously in the wake of liberalisation and globalisation, especially with it's entry in those sectors which were hitherto the domain of the Government. Therefore the time has come to apply the strategy of Gender Budgeting to the private sector.

There is a three fold responsibility that rests with the corporate sector – one of extending the scope of their employment opportunities to more and more women, provide them with level playing fields, equal wages and promotion opportunities; two, to support skill building, training, vocational courses etc; and thirdly, to fulfil their social obligations towards women employees in terms of extending maternity benefits, protection from occupational hazards and sexual harassment, provision of facilities like creches, toilets, sanitation and hygiene, allowing formation of women's associations, legal protection etc.

The civil society organisations whether NGOs, or other community based organisations are partnering government in formulation and implementation of government policies and programmes. Thus their voice and views have an important bearing on shaping economic or social issues pertaining to women. They have to function as 'watch dogs' ensuring that Gender budgeting and mainstreaming is actually taking place right at the grass-root levels and helping in implementing gender concerns effectively.

Informal farm work and non-farm work where women are increasingly employed are mostly non-monetised and therefore cannot be captured in the national accounting system. Despite the sizeable value addition to the national economy, on account of home based and other non-farm and informal activities, the contribution of women's work continues to be invisible. Women also spend considerable time in collecting fuel, fodder, and water and on care related activities, which is neither aid or recognised as an economic activity.

The statistical invisibility of such unpaid work implies that the economic system is missing out on a substantial part of the income generated and value added. The Eleventh Plan should ensure that the National Income includes these activities in their accounting system so that it forms a part of the GDP.

Gender outcome assessment

Gender outcome assessment and evaluation is of utmost importance for ensuring the success of Gender Budgeting. For this it is necessary that the gender fund flow into schemes are properly and correctly assessed. The Finance Ministry has made it mandatory that Gender Outcomes form a part of the Outcome Budget prepared by every Ministry/ Department as part of the Budget documents.

Some anomalies have been observed in allocations reflected in Union Budget 2005-06, under various programmes/schemes for women. In 2005-06 this exercise covered 10 Departments and the total magnitude of Gender Budget was recorded at 2.8 per cent of total Union Government expenditure.

In 2006-07, 24 Departments of the Union Government were included under this exercise and the magnitude of Gender Budget went up to 5.1 per cent of total budget estimates. However, it has been observed that schemes which do not have a 100 per cent women's' component found a mention as women specific schemes. Therefore the first step towards proper outcome assessment of Gender Budget is that each Ministry/Department of both Centre and State should put in place a systematic and comprehensive monitoring and auditing mechanism for outcome assessment. At present, the major task of the Gender Budgeting Cells in the Ministries/ Departments is limited to identification of schemes and computation of allocations meant for women.

In addition to the above, which will primarily be the responsibility of the individual sectorial Ministries/ Departments, the Planning Commission and the Finance Ministry should enable assessment of national level gender outcome assessment through:

— Spatial mapping of gender gaps and resource gaps by Planning Commission;

— Gender audit of public expenditure, programmes and policies;

— There is a need to collect gender desegregated data at national, state and district levels.

Standardisation of data is also necessary to facilitate comparison not only at national but also international levels. The data should flow on a regular basis and should be compiled, collected and analysed periodically.

Bibliography

Abadian, Susan, "Women's Autonomy and its Impact on Fertility", *World Development Vol. 24,* 1996.

Abzug, Bella., and Davis, Susan., "India," *Mapping Progress: Assessing Implementation of the Beijing Platform,* 1998.

Agarwal, Bina, *A Field of One's Own: Gender and Land Rights in South Asia,* Cambridge: Cambridge University Press, 1994.

Anandhi S., "Interlocking Patriarchies and Women in Governance: A Case Study of Panchayati Raj Institutions in Tamil Nadu", in Karin Kapadia, edited *The Violence of Development,* London, Zed Books, 2002.

Arnold, Fred, Kishor Sunita, Roy T. K., "Sex-selective Abortions in India", *Population and Development Review,* 2002.

Arora, D., 'Structural adjustment programmes and gender concerns in India', *Journal of Contemporary Asia,* Vol. 29(3), 1999.

Banerjee, Nirmala, "Women in the Emerging Labour Market", *Indian Journal of Labour Economics, Conference Issue,* 1999.

Basu, Amrita, *Two Faces of Protest: Contrasting Modes of Women's Activism in India,* Berkeley: University of California Press, 1992.

Behrman, Jere R. and Zheng Zhang, "Gender Issues and Employment in Asia", *Asian Development Review,* Vol 13, 1995.

Beneria, Lourdes, "Toward a greater integration of gender in economics", *World Development,* Vol 23, 1995.

Bhat P. N. Mari, "On the Trail of 'Missing' Indian females: Illusion and reality", *Economic and Political Weekly,* 2002.

Bina Agarwal, "Are we not Peasants Too? Land Rights and Women's Claims in Development Resource Centre, UNDP, India, mimeo India, 2002.

Bunch, Charlotte., "The Intolerable Status Quo: Violence Against Women and Girls," *The Progress of Nations,* 1997 New York: UNICEF.

Burns, John F., "Though Illegal, Child Marriage is Popular in Part of India," *The New York Times,* May 11, 1998.

Burns, Nancy, Kay Lehman Scholzman, and Sidney Verba, *The Private Roots of Public Action: Gender, Equality, and Political Participation,* Cambridge, Harvard University Press, 2001.

Carr, Marilyn., and Chen, Martha., and Jhabvala, Renana., *Speaking Out: Women's Economic Empowerment in South Asia,* Southampton Row, London: Intermediate Technology Publications Ltd, 1996.

Chen, M., J. Sebtad and L.O'Connell, "Counting the Invisible Workforce: The Case of Homebased workers', World Development", March 1999.

Desai, Sonalde., *Gender Inequalities and Demographic Behavior: India,* New York: The Population Council, Inc., 1994.

Deshmukh Joy-Ranadive, *Women in Self-Help Groups and Panchayati Raj Institutions: Suggesting Synergistic Linkages,* Occasional paper no 40. New Delhi. CWDS, 2005.

Elson, D., "Labour Markets as Gendered Institutions: Equality, Efficiency and Empowerment Issues", *World Development,* March 1999.

Ghosh, J., "Gender concerns in macro-economic policy", *Economic and Political Weekly,* Vol. 29(18), April 1994.

Gleason, Suzanne, "Female Political Participation and Health in India," *Annals of the American Academy of Political and Social Science,* 2001.

GOI and UNFPA, "Educating Adolescent Girls: Opening Windows, Janshala Joint GOI-UN System Education Programme", New Delhi, 2001.

Government of India, "Mahila Samakhya: Programme for Education for Women's Equality", Ministry of Human Resource Development, Department of Education, New Delhi, 1986.

Govt. of India, "Towards Equality", *Report of the Committee on the Status of Women,* Delhi: Government of India, 1974.

Gurin, Patricia, "Women's Gender Consciousness," *Public Opinion Quarterly,* 1985.

Heise, L., "Violence Against Women: The Hidden Health Burden", *World Bank Discussion Papers,* Washington D.C: 1994.

Indu Prakash Singh, "Indian Women: The Power Trapped" Published by: Galaxy Publications, SFS Flat No.3, Pocket B, Alaknanda, (Ganga Apartments) Kalkaji, New Delhi, 1991.

Jacobson, Doranne and Susan S. Wadley, *Women in India: Two perspectives,* New Delhi: Manohar Publications, 1997.

Jain L.C., "Women Enter Politics", 1992.

Jain S. and A.K. Mathur, "Shiksha Karmi Project: Attempting Nonformalisation of Formal Education", Sandhan Research Centre, Jaipur, 1996.

Jain S. and S. Anandalakshmy, "Shikshakarmi: A Paradigm Shift in the Delivery of Primary Education", Sandhan Research Centre, Jaipur, 1997.

Kishwar, Madhu, "Women and Politics: Beyond Quotas", *Economic and Political Weekly,* XXXI, Number 43, 1996.

Kumari R. Letha, *Women in Politics: Participation in Governance,* New Delhi, Authors Press, 2005.

Mathew, George and Nayak Ramesh C., "Panchayats at Work: What it means for the Oppressed?" *Economic and Political Weekly,* July 6, 1996.

Murthy, Ranjani (eds.), *Building Women's Capacities-Interventions in Gender Transformation,* Sage, New Delhi, 2001.

Nambiar Malini and Bandyopadhyay Kaustuv Kanti, "Self-Help Groups: Engagement with Governance Institutions" in *Participation and Governance,* Volume 10. Number 29, March, 2004.

Neft, Naomi., and Levine, Ann D., *Where Women Stand: An International Report on the Status of Women in 140 Countries,* New York: Random House, 1997.

Niranjana Seemanthini, "Exploring gender Inflections within Panchayati Raj Institutions: Women's Politicisation in Andhra Pradesh", in Karin Kapadia, edited *The Violence of Development,* London, Zed Books, 2002.

Nussbaum, Martha C., "Sex, laws, and inequality: What India can teach the United States," *Daedalus,* 2002..

Okin, Susan Moeller, "Gender, the Public, and the Private," in Anne Phillips ed. *Feminism and Politics,* Oxford; Oxford University Press, 1998.

Omvedt, Gail., "Violence Against Women: New Movements and New Theories in India," *Kali Primaries,* 1990.

Purushothaman, Sangeetha., *The Empowerment of Women in India: Grassroots Women's Networks and the State,* New Delhi: Sage Publications, 1998.

Rajagopal, S. and R.S. Sharma, *Academic Achievement of Children in Angan Pathshalas- A Study,* Institute of Development Studies Research Report, Jaipur, 1997.

Ramalingaswami, Vulimiri., and Jonsson, Urban., and Rohde, Jon., "The Asian Enigma," *The Progress of Nations,* 1996, New York: UNICEF.

Ramesh, Asha and Bharati Ali, "Towards Political Empowerment – Profiling Elected Women Members in Karnataka and Gujarat, (A Report)", 1998.

Standing, Guy, "Global Feminisation Through Flexible Labour: A Theme Revisited", *World Development,* March 1998.

Stree Adhar Kendra, "Women in Decision Making: A Study of Women in Gram Panchayats", 1996.

Thakur, Atanu, "A Post Modernist Enquiry into Women's Workforce Participation", *Indian Journal of Labour Economics,* Conference Issue, Vol. 42, 1999.

Tinker, Anne., *Improving Women's Health in India,* Development in Practice Series. The World Bank, 1996.

Unni, Jeemol and Uma Rani, "Informal Sector: Women in the Emerging Labour Market", *The Indian Journal of Labour Economics,* 42(4), October-December, 1999.

Venkateswaran, Sandhya., *Environment, Development and the Gender Gap,* New Delhi: Sage Publications, 1995.

Vinayak, Ramesh, "Victims of Sudden Affluence," *India Today,* December 15, 1997.

Index

All India Coordinated Research Project (AICRP) 147
All-India Women's Conference (AIWC) 200

Bharatiya Janata Party (BJP) 209
Bihar Institute of Economic Studies (BIES) 99
Brahmo Samaj Marriage Act 11

Canadian International Development Agency (CIDA) 100
Caste system 28
Child Marriage Restraint Act 15
Committee on the Status of Women in India (CSWI) 201
Constitutional Amendment Act 198
Constitutional Amendment Gram Panchayats 222

Department of Rural Development (DRD) 225
Disaster management policy 258
District Development Committee (DDC) 224
District Planning Committee 219
Domestic Violence Act 260
Dowry Prohibition Act 13

Export-oriented industrialisation 156

Family Resource Management 148
Fourth World Conference on Women 76

Gender Budgeting Cells 253
Globalisation 156

Hindu Widow Marriage Act 15
Homogenous category 238
Hunter Commission 37

Indian electoral politics 214
Indian National Congress 199
Indian Penal Code (IPC) 13
Individual sectorial policies 259
Information and Communication Technology (ICT) 74, 98
Information Technology (IT) 100
Intellectual Revolution 17
International Classification of Status in Employment (ICSE) 157

Krishi Vigyan Kendra (KVK) 145

Law-enforcing agencies 242
Liberalisation 154
Livestock management 142
Look East policy 241

Material nourishment 25

Maternal health programmes 247
Maternity Benefit Act 259, 260
Minimum Wages Act 260
Ministry of Women and Child Development (MWCD) 251
Muslim Code of Conduct 12

National Assessment and Accreditation Council (NAAC) 78
National Bank of Agriculture and Rural Development (NABARD) 100
National Common Minimum Programme 249
National Education System 79
National macro-economic policies 254
National Revolutionary Council 193
National Rural Employment Guarantee Scheme 256
National Sample Survey Organisation (NSSO) 84
Non-Timber Forest Products (NTFP) 143

Other Backward Classes (OBCs) 209

Poverty alleviation programmes 256
Prenatal Diagnostic Technique 260

Re-vitalisation 73
Rural Infrastructure Development Fund (RIDF) 100

Seethalakshmi Ramaswamy College for Women (SRCW) 101
Self-Help Groups of Women (SHG) 145
Social security insurance schemes 257
Sovereign Democratic Secular Government 29
Special Marriage Act 11
Structural adjustment programme 156
Subject Matter Specialists (SMS) 146
Swadeshi movement 192

Tantra philosophy 20

Universal elementary education 76
Upanishadic period 30

Watershed Development Trusts (WDTs) 223
Weak law enforcement 229
Wide Area Network (WAN) 146
Women's Component Plan (WCP) 252
World Food Programme 6

Zilla Parishad 70